BE QUICK—
BUT DON'T HURRY!

FINDING SUCCESS IN THE
TEACHINGS OF A LIFETIME

ANDREW HILL
WITH JOHN WOODEN

SIMON & SCHUSTER

New York   London   Toronto   Sydney

SIMON & SCHUSTER
Rockefeller Center
1230 Avenue of the Americas
New York, NY 10020

SIMON & SCHUSTER and colophon are registered trademarks
of Simon & Schuster, Inc.

Book design by Ellen R. Sasahara

Manufactured in the United States of America

19 20 18

Library of Congress Cataloging-in-Publication Data is available

ISBN 0-7432-1388-2

To my Mom, for all her love.

To Janice, Alex, and Aaron for all their support.

To Coach, for all his wisdom.

CONTENTS

FOREWORD
BY JOHN WOODEN

THE PYRAMID OF SUCCESS is the result of my trying to develop something that would make me a better teacher as well as give those under my supervision something to aspire to other than a higher grade in my English class or more points in an athletic contest. In 1934 I coined my own definition of success: "Peace of mind which is a direct result of self-satisfaction in knowing you made the effort to do the best of which you are capable." However, after a period of time, I came to the conclusion that since a definition is often difficult for a student to comprehend, something visual would be a more effective communication tool. I then came up with the idea of a Pyramid of Success. I spent as much time as possible over the next fourteen years in selecting those personal traits and characteristics that I think are essential in enabling one to reach success according to my definition. After selecting a trait for each block, much time was spent in getting each block strategically placed in the structure.

Whether in the classroom or on the basketball court, the principles contained in the Pyramid were central to

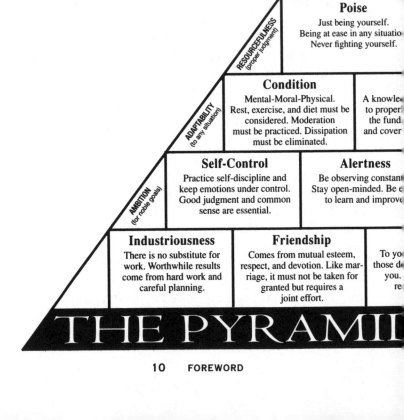

FAITH
(through prayer)

FIGHT
(determined effort)

RESOURCEFULNESS
(proper judgment)

ADAPTABILITY
(to any situation)

AMBITION
(for noble goals)

Competi

Be at you
is ne
a di

Poise

Just being yourself.
Being at ease in any situatio
Never fighting yourself.

Condition

Mental-Moral-Physical.
Rest, exercise, and diet must be
considered. Moderation
must be practiced. Dissipation
must be eliminated.

A knowle
to proper
the fund
and cover

Self-Control

Practice self-discipline and
keep emotions under control.
Good judgment and common
sense are essential.

Alertness

Be observing constan
Stay open-minded. Be e
to learn and improve

Industriousness

There is no substitute for
work. Worthwhile results
come from hard work and
careful planning.

Friendship

Comes from mutual esteem,
respect, and devotion. Like marriage, it must not be taken for
granted but requires a
joint effort.

To yo
those de
you.
re

THE PYRAMI

PATIENCE
(good things take time)

...eatness
...n your best
...oyment of
...llenge.

INTEGRITY
(purity of intention)

Confidence
...espect without fear. May come
...om being prepared and keeping
...ll things in proper perspective.

RELIABILITY
(creates respect)

...the ability
...kly execute
...Be prepared
...e detail.

Team Spirit
A genuine consideration for
others. An eagerness to
sacrifice personal interests of
glory for the welfare of all.

HONESTY
(in thought and action)

Initiative
...ltivate the ability to make
...ecisions and think alone.
...o not be afraid of failure,
but learn from it.

Intentness
Set a realistic goal. Concentrate
on its achievement by resisting
all temptations and being
determined and persistent.

SINCERITY
(keeps friends)

...y
...to all
...upon
...r self-

Cooperation
With all levels of your
coworkers. Listen if you want
to be heard. Be interested in
finding the best way, not in
having your own way.

Enthusiasm
Brushes off upon those with
whom you come in contact.
You must truly enjoy what
you are doing.

OF SUCCESS

my teaching process. By simply listing the blocks, you will see how they are all related to successful team play: enthusiasm, cooperation, loyalty, friendship, industriousness, intentness, initiative, alertness, self-control, team spirit, skill, condition, poise, confidence, and competitive greatness. Athletics, when viewed as an integral part of a university's goal of educating young men and women, must be about more than just winning and losing games. It must be about teaching those traits necessary for succeeding in life.

Ultimately, it is the goal of every teacher and coach that their students take the lessons they have learned in the classroom and on the athletic field and apply them in their lives after graduation. Indeed, a teacher can receive no higher compliment than to see former students integrate those lessons into the fabric of their lives. This book, written by one former student, gives me special pleasure because the author not only studied hard but took the concepts and elements of my teachings and added his own experiences to envision the lessons in ways that go beyond the original teachings. There is nothing more satisfying for a teacher than watching his students make his lessons their own.

I

LEARNING

GROWING UP as a sports-crazed kid in Westwood, California, I had the chance to watch some of the nation's most compelling stars and teams compete in my own backyard. The Dodgers with Sandy Koufax and Don Drysdale, and the Lakers with Jerry West and Elgin Baylor were fun to watch as they battled for world championships, but they were not the most successful teams in town. That distinction belonged to a college team just a couple of miles from my house: During the 1960s and 1970s, Coach John Wooden's UCLA Bruins were the most dominant and successful sports program ever seen.

Coach Wooden's UCLA basketball teams were a high-speed, classy, Blue-and-Gold winning machine. While it's hard to imagine that integration was still an issue in college basketball back then, those Bruins were somewhat in the vanguard, with their perfect blend of black and white, urban and rural, big and small. The starters were a black center from Kansas, two white kids from Southern California, a black guard from Philadelphia, and a Jewish forward born in Brooklyn. UCLA won its first NCAA championship in 1964, two full years before an all-black Texas Western (now University of Texas El Paso) team beat an all-white University of Kentucky team and hastened the recruitment of black ballplayers at every school in the country. The Bruins played with a consistency and controlled passion that seemed a direct reflection of their coach. The culture of Los Angeles in the 1960s was so self-consciously hip that John Wooden's provincial Indiana roots made him appear to be from another planet. Unlike the style-conscious L.A. glitterati, he was very secure in who he was and where he came from. In a city where everyone wanted to be cool, this man clearly had no interest in imitating the world of movie deals, cutting-edge fashion, rock music, and air kisses. If Pat Riley was the quintessence of L.A. style as coach of the Lakers in the 1980s, Coach Wooden was its antithesis, bringing to the limelight the solid Midwestern values of substance over Showtime. Even as a young boy I could sense that there was something special about a man like this; John Wooden was "cool" simply because he didn't try to fit in and conform to the shifting tides of Southern California culture.

This is not to say his teams were boring. The Bruins were built on speed, quickness, a tough man-to-man defense, a withering zone press, and a relentless fast break. Now, there may be some kid in America who grows up dreaming of playing slow-down, highly structured, Princeton-style basketball, but I've never met that kid. There was something intoxicating and captivating about the pace and attacking style of the Bruins. Many of their games were close and hard fought, but then the Bruins would generate a blistering run that devastated the opposition, the basketball equivalent of a heavyweight boxer knocking out his opponent. I was already a fan before the Bruins won their first national title in 1963–64, but that season pushed my infatuation to new heights.

Though the players changed through the years, the sense of style and class that came to epitomize UCLA basketball always grew out of the concepts espoused by Coach Wooden. Central to those teachings was his Pyramid of Success, which is familiar to the tens of millions of sports fans who marveled at this remarkable sports dynasty. The Pyramid was Coach Wooden's attempt to diagram the key ingredients necessary for personal success (see diagram pages 10–11). With a foundation based on qualities like industriousness, friendship, loyalty, cooperation, and enthusiasm, the Pyramid builds to an apex that is capped off with patience and faith. To those who have never met Coach Wooden, it seems almost too corny to be true.

But Coach doesn't just act square, he *is* square. His body may be shrinking with age, but his place in the pantheon of American heroes only grows with each passing year. In a world where everyone else seems desperate for fifteen minutes of fame, Coach somewhat grudgingly accepts celebrity while never seeming quite comfortable in the spotlight's glare. This is a man who learned many of his early lessons from the stories his father would read to him by the light of a coal oil lamp in their electricity-free farmhouse near Centerton, Indiana. It is no coincidence that the qualities he prescribes in his Pyramid of Success pretty accurately describe Coach himself. He is an American icon who reminds us all that the pursuit of success does not require that you compromise your morals and values.

Fewer than two hundred men have had the opportunity to work extensively with Coach in his favorite class-room, the basketball court. I was fortunate enough to be one of those men. Like all the great pyramids of the world, the Wooden Pyramid is remarkable not only for its strength and symmetry, but also for the secrets hidden on the inside. Pyramids do not readily give up their hidden treasures to those without a sense of adventure and a will-ingness to travel down dangerous and dimly lit passage-ways. But with persistence and an inclination to learn from past mistakes, an intrepid explorer can shed light on the treasures within, and it has been my privilege to be one such explorer.

The secrets of the Wooden Pyramid are simple, re-markably easy to follow, and available to anyone wishing to "own" them. These secrets are absolutely guaranteed to make you better at managing any business, team, or organization. They will help you in your home life, in your relationships with people, and in your understand-ing of all group processes. As one might expect from Coach Wooden, there was never an attempt to conceal these secrets; they were always hidden in plain sight. So in a sense, the odyssey of discovery that I will share with you is sort of embarrassing.

I had been away from basketball and Coach Wooden for nearly twenty-five years before I realized that virtually everything I believed in and used in my professional life was derived from my years of playing a simple game that comes down to throwing a ball through a hoop. I was al-most chagrined the day I had the epiphany that sent me running back to see Coach with my great revelation—that every lesson I learned playing basketball had led di-rectly to my success in business. Was I just dense, or was this the way Coach planned it all along? To find out, let's go back to where my journey began.

BASEBALL was my passion until the early 1960s, when John Wooden's UCLA Bruins became my favorite team. They played a fast, unselfish, and appealing style of basketball, and it was surprisingly easy to get a ticket. Though Coach had been promised an on-campus arena when the school brought him out from Indiana in 1948, that promise remained unfulfilled for nearly twenty years while the Bruins played their home games all over Los Angeles. As long as you were willing to travel to a variety of sites like the Pan Pacific Auditorium, Venice High School, and Santa Monica City College, you could get a great seat to a Bruin home game. John Wooden was a well-respected coach with a consistent winning record and a reputation as a fine teacher of the game—and then in 1964, the Bruins, with no player taller than 6'5", employed a full-court press on their way to a 30-0 record and their first NCAA championship. Coach Wooden was all of a sudden the sports world's latest genius . . . and I was totally hooked on basketball.

I spent countless hours in my small backyard, shooting hoops with the Bruin fight song playing over and over in my mind. With the clock ticking down toward zero, I hit millions of game-winning shots while I was still a teenager. Coach Wooden's Bruins were my heroes, led by their kindly old Coach (pretty scary that I am now the same age he was when he first entered my consciousness). But playing for the Bruins did not seem to be even a remote possibility in my early teens; my sights were set on making the team at University High School, where the

coach was a former Bruin player from the 1950s, Courtney Borio.

My high school years were improbably happy ones, as
I made the basketball team as a sophomore, and then
made All-League as a junior. Needless to say, in that time I
attended every single Bruin home game, and was a regular from the minute Pauley Pavilion opened in 1966.
While most of my high school classmates spent their
summers lounging at the nearby beaches, mine were
spent in the hot and decrepit gym at Uni High. Those
long days of endless games were true athletic bliss. The
best were when we would have five or six hours of tough,
competitive games in the gym, followed by a more formal, officiated evening game against a local high school. I
lived, ate, and slept basketball. A burning desire to improve combined with an insatiable love of the game made
the hard work seem like play. The hours of practice paid
off, and I developed into a gifted high school player.

My senior year in high school far exceeded my wildest
hopes. I averaged over 27 points, 12 assists, and 5 rebounds a game, as our team went undefeated in our
league and almost won the City title. I was named to the
All-City team and was the top player in our league. Coach
Courtney Borio had played, sparingly, at UCLA in the
early 1950s. It was clear he held Coach Wooden in the
highest regard; though he never overtly tried to influence
me, I could tell that he really hoped I would try to make
my mark at UCLA. Two of my former high school teammates, John Ecker and Bill Seibert, were already enrolled
at UCLA with basketball scholarships, so I had built-in
buddies in the program. Dozens of colleges came after
me, but they were all a blur when it became clear that a

scholarship at UCLA was in the cards. The first time I went to campus to meet Coach Wooden after practice, I could barely speak I was in such awe. He seemed so humble and gentle, sort of like the kindly grandfather who drove the wagon in the old Pepperidge Farm commercials. Sitting at training table between Coach Wooden and Kareem Abdul-Jabbar (who was still using the name Lew Alcindor at this point) was so thrilling I felt like I was living a dream.

I now understand that this dreamlike state set in motion by the recruiting process is probably at the root of much of the pain and disappointment that young ballplayers experience when their dreams of starring in college never come to pass. Most young men I knew in the 1960s had fathers who were obsessed with work. Women's liberation was still a nascent concept, and in most families it was the mother's job to raise the kids. Some kids I knew had fathers who were workaholics, some were alcoholics, but not many of them were All-American fathers. My dad was no exception. But most college basketball coaches fit the mold of the father every kid wished he had (Bobby Knight is an obvious exception here), so if my own father was largely absent . . . big deal. I could always find that gentle, strong, nurturing father when I picked the college coach I was going to play for. All of this played itself out subconsciously when I was a teenager. There was nothing wrong with wanting a warm, caring, masculine father—but in retrospect, I see that it's a mistake to think that the place to find him was on the basketball court.

Unlike most of the coaches I spoke to in the recruiting process, Coach Wooden made no promises beyond an opportunity to play and access to a great education. He didn't tell me how much the Bruins needed me, nor did he guarantee me playing time. It was clear from my earliest contacts with Coach Wooden that he was different from his peers; he seemed not only more secure (a few national titles under your belt will do that), but also more centered as a person. He clearly wanted me to come to UCLA, but there was absolutely no sense that he *needed* me to attend. It wasn't just me: It didn't matter if you were Kareem Abdul-Jabbar, Bill Walton, or Andy Hill, the feeling you got from John Wooden in the recruiting process was that he would be "pleased" if you came, but he would lose no sleep it you went somewhere else. To this day, Coach brags that he never contacted an out-of-state ballplayer unless they wrote to him first, which is hard to imagine given today's frenzied recruiting. But I didn't need anyone to beg me to play for the Bruins; it was my most outlandish hope to get the chance to wear the Blue and Gold, and I wasn't about to let the opportunity slip through my fingers just because playing time might be hard to come by. Better to pursue a dream and fail than to have never tried. Or so I thought. After briefly flirting with the idea of going to Stanford, I found the lure of playing for John Wooden in Pauley Pavilion far too powerful, and I committed to attending UCLA. I knew it was a big decision, but at seventeen years old, it was hard to imagine how this decision would impact my life—in good ways and bad—for decades to come.

John Wooden seemed to be the perfect fit for the father figure I so strongly craved. My own father's alcoholism made family life pretty unpleasant; this friendly, teetotaling churchgoer from Indiana seemed the polar opposite of my biological father in every way imaginable. My contact with my father was pretty infrequent, so it seemed logical to hope that I could fill the void with someone who would be a daily presence. After all, players spent hours every day with their coach. Needless to say, while I was looking for a nurturing and kindly father, Coach Wooden was simply looking for his next great guard. He already had a son and a daughter, and lots of grandchildren, and this father figure fantasy was strictly a one-way affair.

In the 1968–69 season, freshmen could not play on the varsity, so I was paired in the backcourt on our freshman team with Henry Bibby (now the very bald head coach at USC). The freshman coach was Gary Cunningham, a former Bruin star who is now athletic director at the University of California at Santa Barbara. The drills we ran and the philosophies employed were identical to those of the varsity. The emphasis on fundamentals was amazing. I averaged almost 20 points and 8 assists, and I shared with Henry the Seymour Armond Award given to the most valuable freshman player. I got to see my name on a trophy that included legendary Bruin players, like Kareem Abdul-Jabbar, Mike Warren, and Gail Goodrich, who were my heroes growing up; I was certain that my own legend was just beginning. Pauley Pavilion at UCLA was still pretty new, but championship banners hung from every corner; now it was going to be my turn to help hang more of those banners from the rafters. For a nineteen-year-old kid from Westwood, life doesn't get much better than this.

My freshman year went so well that they even asked me to help recruit an incoming player, a junior in high school who had a brother who was a great football player. The recruit was a shy, sixteen-year-old stuttering giant named Bill Walton. Bill was so shy that he had trouble making eye contact, and had so much difficulty speaking that his words tumbled out softly in an unintelligible mumble. We had a great dinner (after I convinced young Bill that he really could order a steak instead of hamburger), and a fun night at a Laker game. I may have only participated in recruiting one player, but he turned out to be one of the great players of all time.

With fall fast approaching, I was going to have the opportunity to make my childhood wishes come true. Of course, with the graduation of the great Kareem Abdul-Jabbar along with a host of other star players, no one was predicting another national championship for UCLA. Kareem had led the Bruins to three straight titles and an astonishing record of 88-2. The expectation around the country was that the Bruins' domination of college basketball was about to end; it was going to be a chance for all the schools that had lost to UCLA in the past few years to even the score. The stakes were high, and the anticipation intense, but finally formal varsity basketball practice was going to begin. Thirty years have passed, but I still get butterflies in my stomach just thinking about it.

As a sophomore at UCLA in 1969, I didn't waste much time before putting Coach and myself at loggerheads. In fact, I probably set some sort of record with how quickly I managed to anger him. Sometimes historical events and personal aspirations can crash together in ways that almost seem predestined; October 15, 1969, was to be one such day. It was not only my very first day of official varsity basketball practice; it was also the day of the first national student moratorium to protest the war in Vietnam. It seemed pretty obvious to me that as concerned student-athletes, we should stand side by side with other students in protesting the war. In those days, it was tough to find *anyone* on a university campus who supported our country's policies in the war. Being young, self-righteous, and exceedingly cocky, I felt little hesitation in moving forward with my "brilliant" plan: I went to my two closest friends on the basketball team, John Ecker and Terry Schofield, and asked them to come with me to see Coach Wooden so we could ask him to call off practice in support of the Vietnam moratorium. Terry was smart enough to know that this was a colossally dumb idea, and he turned me down on the spot. In fact, Terry thought I was completely out of my mind. Turns out, he was right. John, after much coaxing, agreed to come along.

Further indication of my own naïveté is that I thought it was *an added bonus* that our first day of practice was also national media day. Hundreds of reporters from around the country would attend practice, take pictures, and ask questions; they were all anxious to cover what everyone presumed would be the Bruins' demise now that we had lost Kareem Abdul-Jabbar to the professional ranks. Everyone was pretty tired of the Bruins' dynasty, and watching it fall was worth plenty of coverage. Being the kind of know-it-all that only a nineteen-year-old can be, I thought this was a perfect opportunity to use the media to make the world aware how concerned student-athletes felt about the war in Southeast Asia. I was filled with moral certitude and self-righteousness as John Ecker and I went to see Coach Wooden. Surely he would be impressed by our strong feelings and offer his support.

Coach's door was always open, and a couple of hours before practice was scheduled to start, John and I walked in to see him. John Ecker was at least smart enough to let me do the talking, and I laid out my idea with great enthusiasm.

After a brief speech outlining my objections to the war, I offered a suggestion that Coach Wooden call off practice in support of the student moratorium. I thought the speech went pretty well, and I fully expected to get Coach's support; at the very least, I expected some sort of sympathy-tinged regret that expressed his agreement with our ideals while rejecting my plan. After all, he had listened attentively. But the response was far short of what I had hoped for. Coach simply said, "Andy, *you* don't have to come to practice . . . you don't *ever* have to come to practice. But there is no way that I am calling off practice for this moratorium." He then went on to pretty well blister John and me for our political beliefs, leaving us to decide what we wanted to do.

I was stunned and saddened by his reaction. At last, I had met someone at UCLA who supported our country's position in Vietnam. What an uncomfortable revelation! Here I had spent my whole life dreaming of playing for John Wooden's Bruins, and on my very first day of practice I had completely ticked him off. Not a great career move to say the least. John and I struggled with the choice between acting forcefully on our principles or pursuing our lifelong dream. A difficult choice for any man . . . and we were just a couple of college boys. But were we willing to place our political convictions above our basketball careers? Each option had a personal cost.

Of course, John and I swallowed our political pride

and showed up to practice with the rest of the squad. I had worked hard for years to be in a position to compete for a spot on the UCLA basketball team. Yet as I walked out on the floor for my first practice, instead of goose bumps and an adrenaline high, I had the somber feeling that I had wimped out on something far more important than basketball. Our pride and sense of personal integrity had been deeply wounded by choosing our personal dreams over our principles. Guys our age were fighting and dying halfway around the globe, while we were safe and sound, going to school for free with an athletic scholarship and protected by our student draft deferments. Probably not the best state of mind for a young man facing the greatest physical challenge of his lifetime, but once practice started it was all behind us. To his credit, Wooden never brought the topic up again, unlike some coaches who probably would have needled me mercilessly for my preposterous request. And to my credit, I decided to keep my political views out of the basketball arena—at least for a while.

Preseason practice at UCLA was physically demanding and extremely competitive. From day one, Henry Bibby was simply fantastic, and it soon became clear that he was going to be a major contributor. Whether I was going to get much playing time was much murkier; Coach usually only played seven guys, and by the time our six-week preseason had concluded, even ignoring my political run-in with Coach, my chances of making the rotation seemed pretty shaky. Then, ever so briefly, the picture took a drastic and surprising turn for the better. Our first game at Pauley Pavilion was an intrasquad game, and I was the star of the night. Coach Wooden was quoted in the newspaper saying that against certain defenses I might actually be the team's top guard. I could hardly believe this was happening. There was my name in the headline of the *Los Angeles Times,* while the now defunct *Herald-Examiner* called me a potential "right-handed Gail Goodrich." (Goodrich had been an All-American at UCLA and was an NBA All-Star.) Walking to class up Bruin Walk, I was warmly greeted by football players, pretty girls, and professors of unknown subjects. How was I to know that I was already in my fifteenth minute of fame?

On the strength of my performance in that intrasquad game, I got a few opportunities early in my sophomore year to get into games before the outcome was decided. But I never really got comfortable, always felt nervous, and once conference play started my playing time was limited to garbage time at the end of blowout wins. Having been a star in high school and in my freshman year at UCLA, I found sitting and watching a tough adjustment to make. But great high school or freshman players don't always make great college varsity players. Fortunately, we were winning, and somehow winning makes it hard to complain. It was also fun to be a part of a squad as it builds up confidence; we literally found ourselves laughing toward the end of games as we wondered what unexpected event would lead to the next Bruin win. Keep in mind that, post-Abdul-Jabbar, we were *not* supposed to win every game, so it was really fun to surprise the country, who hoped that the Bruins would finally fall off the championship throne.

One game I remember vividly from that year was a close one that was decided by John Ecker, who was used regularly but sparingly as our seventh man. It was early in our conference season, and we were playing Oregon State at home. This was a game that everyone expected us to win easily, but the Beavers were a pesky group, and we actually trailed 71–70 late in the game. With the clock running down and the Bruins working for a final shot, a double foul was called out on the floor and Sidney Wicks, our All American starting forward, fouled out with 16 seconds left in the game. Oregon State called a quick time-out. The capacity crowd in Pauley Pavilion was in a frenzied state of anxiety. To put this situation in perspective, since moving into Pauley Pavilion five seasons earlier, UCLA had compiled a home record of 60-1. These fans just were not used to being on the short end of the score. The Bruins came over to the sidelines, and our coaches put their heads together in conference. The sense I had on the bench is that no one much wanted to enter a game with this little time remaining. We'd all been sitting for a long time, and had cold legs, so we avoided eye contact with Coach and prayed we wouldn't get put in the game.

As Coach surveyed his bench, his two top subs and my best friends on the team, John Ecker and Terry Schofield, looked at each other and simultaneously exclaimed, "I hope it's you!" The horn to start the action sounded, and amazingly Coach Wooden had forgotten to put *anyone* into the game. As the remaining four Bruins walked out on the floor, Coach falsely assumed that the player he put into the game had to jump for possession (which was actually not the case), and at the last instant he put in the taller Ecker. John ran on the floor, got the tap over to Curtis Rowe and curled into the lane. Steve Patterson had the ball at the high post, spotted Ecker, and delivered a perfect pass to John. John faked his man right, turned left, and hit a short jump-hook for a 72–71 win! Just like in practice. Man, that place exploded. Sidney Wicks ran on the floor and picked John up and held him there, suspended in time and the joy of the last-second victory.

What made this moment stay so clear in my memory is what happened the next day: I had stopped in at the "hero's" house to go out and celebrate, and just as I stepped in John's front door, the phone rang. It was my dad calling to congratulate John, a sweet gesture that seemed so out of character we were both amazed. Neither one of us had a dad who did much in the way of encouraging us in any way. John's father had disappeared from his life when he was a youngster, and my alcoholic and emotionally abusive dad was just not the sort of guy to spontaneously do something nice. He had never called John before . . . and never called him again after that. I'm not sure he ever congratulated *me* for anything. But it was a memorable moment in a strange, awful, and wonderful sophomore season, and a somehow bitter underscore that made us both aware of how little our fathers had to do with our lives.

The season was not totally without adversity, and toward the end of the 1969–70 schedule we actually lost a couple of games. In one game, at Oregon, there were over four thousand students who couldn't get in to watch the game who watched on closed circuit TV in a campus auditorium. The Oregon team was hot all night, and they beat us handily. Players met in groups late into the night, getting buried feelings off our chests and resolving to work closer as a team. Then, a few games later, our crosstown rivals USC came in to Pauley Pavilion and beat us by a point. Those losses actually did bring us closer as a team, and probably helped when NCAA tournament time came around. By season's end, our talented team was 28-2, culminating in a dramatic win in the national championship game over Artis Gilmore's Jacksonville team.

Despite the team's success, my sophomore year was an unhappy, disillusioning time. Coach Wooden paid little attention to the reserves in practice, and even less attention to our psychological needs off the floor. We were fodder for the starters; if I made a great play in practice, Coach would focus his attention on how the first-team player could have "permitted" something like this to happen. It was fun to win a national championship, but not as much fun as most people would think. When you've been a star player your whole life, suddenly sitting on the bench and watching the action is pretty painful. Far from the spotlight you had in high school, you suffer as your family and friends on the East Coast complain that they had to stay up watching TV until one in the morning before you got into the game. You come off the bench cold, and by the time you're warm you are headed for the showers. While most of my parents' friends were amazed that a little guy like me was even close to playing for the vaunted Bruins, it was hard for me to feel that way; I badly wanted to play, and youth clouded my ability to judge my own talent. When you feel overlooked and unappreciated it can be pretty depressing. And when the person overlooking you is someone you idolize, like John Wooden, the lack of attention can be devastating. Surprisingly, I found out years later that even some of the star players felt that Coach gave them less positive attention than they craved. But stars had adoring fans and newspaper head-lines to stroke their egos, while the benchwarmers were left to fend for themselves.

The annual Bruin basketball banquet that year was a festive affair attended by thousands of rabid fans. Sports fans always like it when their team wins, but they go absolutely wild when their underdog squad goes all the way, so this championship was especially sweet for the Bruin basketball faithful. The banquet hall was overflowing with passionate fans and good cheer for most of the evening. But events took a dramatic and unexpected turn. In addition to the usual awards and highlight films, each of the graduating players was given the opportunity to make a speech. One of those players, Bill Seibert, my teammate at University High School, blistered Coach Wooden in his speech. He talked about what he perceived to be the unfair treatment of the reserves on the team, and was highly critical of Coach. Bill and some other reserves had been suspended for a pillow fight, while a few of the starters had been caught doing far worse with minimal consequences. Needless to say, the crowd at the Beverly Hilton Hotel did not come to hear something like this; Bill's speech was about as popular as if he'd ripped the Pope from his balcony in the Vatican. Scattered boos were heard throughout the banquet hall.

Just below the dais where we were seated, Seibert's family sat at their front-row table in astonishment. As Bill went on and the crowd grew more uncomfortable, Bill's father hollered at Bill to sit down, and his mother quietly cried. It was a totally surreal scene. But when Bill finished his speech, the entire team, including starting players Sidney Wicks, Curtis Rowe, Steve Patterson, John Vallely, and Henry Bibby, rose and gave him an ovation. In a day and age when the common rallying cry at universities across the country was "power to the people," Bill had taken his brief moment in the spotlight to question a man who seemed beyond reproach. Though many on the team disagreed with Bill's timing and choice of venue, we all admired his courage. And on a purely personal level, I must admit I was silently relieved that for a change someone else was opening his big mouth besides me. What had to be said was being said, but this time I managed to stay out of Coach Wooden's line of fire . . . or so I thought.

The following Monday, I got a message as I was leaving my Political Science class that Coach Wooden wanted to see me in his office. That was pretty unusual, and I had no idea what he needed to speak to me about. When I arrived, Coach Wooden, along with his assistants Denny Crum and Gary Cunningham, were gathered on one side of the office. Much to my astonishment, Coach told me that if I agreed with Bill Seibert, I should leave school. They would be happy to make some calls to help me transfer. I was stunned. Later that day, I found out that they had the same meeting with my two closest pals on the team, John Ecker and Terry Schofield. All three of us turned them down on their invitation to leave, but we were all badly shaken. We may have wished we were playing more, but none of us had any interest in playing anywhere but UCLA. (Ironically, Coach Wooden actually got Bill Seibert a job after he left UCLA. More than a few of us thought it was somewhat amusing that the job Coach found for Bill was in Tasmania, the remote but beautiful island off the southern coast of Australia. If you wanted to put a guy "out to pasture" and still look like a nice guy, getting him a job in Tasmania would be the perfect solution. Coach Wooden could teach Tony Soprano a thing or two about how to gracefully eliminate a problem.)

The fact that John, Terry, and I had somehow been singled out by our coaches and asked to leave really riled up our teammates. It was incredibly gratifying that everyone got behind us; we actually had discussions about renting a room off campus at a local hotel and inviting Coach to come over for a meeting with the team to discuss our concerns about his heavy-handed tactics. But Coach got wind of our plan, and co-opted it by arranging for a meeting in the athletic director's office. The players never got the opportunity to meet and plan a strategy, and we all went to the meeting with no sense of the agenda or what was going to be discussed. Somehow, a rumor had started that we were going to confront Coach with an extensive list of demands; in truth, there was no list. Another rumor popped up that Coach would resign before he capitulated to our demands; the truth was, we had no demands, just some concerns we wanted to put on the table. But the air of tension and distrust was thick as the meeting was called to order.

Coach opened the meeting by saying that he had heard that there were some rumblings, and he wanted everything out on the table. Then he opened the floor and asked for comments. Once again, I was dumb enough to jump in and have my say. I talked about how miserable it felt to be singled out, that it would be nice if every once in a while he would positively acknowledge that a second-stringer did something right instead of ignoring everything we did. I also added that he needed to know that we all thought he was a tremendous coach. A couple of other guys added some brief comments, and then an awkward silence came over the room. We had just won the national championship, and here we were, a bunch of whining, complaining kids. The athletic director, J.D. Morgan, was clearly peeved at us. In hindsight, I don't blame him. No one knew what direction the meeting was going to take next. What was J.D. going to do? What was Coach going to say? You could have cut the tension with a knife.

Then something truly memorable happened that not only changed the course of the meeting, but also probably set us up for our championship run the following year. Though our team was evenly divided between black and white players, the truth was that most of our friendships were with guys who looked like us. Off the court, the black guys went their way and the white guys went theirs. In the middle of the season just concluded, the black members of the team asked to resegregate the team on road trips because they were more comfortable rooming with their black teammates. This was a difficult and confusing period for all of us, and the potential for a racial divide seemed omnipresent. So here we were questioning the most successful coach in the country, and the flashpoint of this meeting had been three white guys, none of them All-Americans. At that moment, our best player (and probably the best player in the country) was an articulate and charismatic black man named Sidney Wicks. At 6'8½" and 235 pounds, Sidney was the first truly athletic, fast power forward to play the game. Sidney stood up and addressed Coach. The gist of what Sidney said was that he couldn't understand why Coach Wooden would feel so threatened by our group's need to address some problems. After all, it was Coach Wooden who had taught us what it meant to be a part of a team, taught us to back up our teammates, and taught us that if we stood together we could beat anybody. It was clear that even Coach Wooden was moved by Sidney's powerful argument. Though he said little in response, even Coach had to smile in recognition of the truth of Sidney's statement. Suddenly, the tension was diffused, the anger subsided, and shortly thereafter we were all back on campus laughing and joking like a bunch of college teammates should. But I will never forget Sidney's courage in a tough spot. He really saved the day.

The way Coach ran the UCLA basketball program was not the only thing being questioned by the rebellious youth of America in 1970. The antiwar movement was raging, and university campuses all around the country were being shut down by strikes. Not surprisingly many team members were swept up in the spirit of protest that affected students and united millions of activists from every state in the union. As President Nixon escalated the war into Laos and Cambodia, and the administration's hostility toward protesters became more overt, it seemed appropriate to use the media to try to make our leadership understand that not all students against the war were hippies and anarchists. What better way to do that than to have the clean-cut national basketball champions write a letter voicing their concerns? Sidney Wicks's dramatic speech in J.D. Morgan's office had made us closer as a team than we had ever been during our recent championship season, and expressing political unity was just an extension of who we were as student-athletes. When an alumnus with close ties to the basketball program informed me that President Nixon's closest adviser was a big Bruin hoops fan, it seemed natural to write to the President in care of Mr. H.R. "Bob" Haldeman. At the time, none of us had ever heard of H.R. Haldeman; this was before the Watergate scandal made him a household name. But if he could get a letter to President Nixon, it seemed too good an opportunity to pass up. As students protected by our draft deferments, it seemed the least we could do on behalf of our contemporaries who were fighting and dying overseas.

We all met at a guesthouse in Brentwood that a powerful alumnus rented out to Steve Patterson, our starting center. Not all the ballplayers were politically active, but a few of us were passionate about using whatever influence we might have to put an end to the war. We spent hours crafting a strongly worded, fairly radical letter to the President. After many debates over the wording, the letter was mailed to Mr. Haldeman. Not content to simply sign the letter as individuals, we identified the signers as "U.C.L.A. 1970 N.C.A.A. Basketball Champions." Not exactly subtle, were we? One of the signers (I never found out who, nor does it matter) took a copy and showed it to Coach. It would be the height of understatement to say he was not pleased! So what did Coach do? Once again, he called me into his office for a "chat." "Why did you write this letter?" he asked. "Come on, Coach, everyone wrote and signed that letter," I suggested innocently. But Coach wasn't buying my line, and he responded, "Andy, you and I both know this was your idea, and it sounds to me like you wrote it." Every fiber of my body wanted to plead my case. After all, who was he to accuse me like this? But Coach was basically correct. And for once, logic overcame my righteous indignation. I didn't even argue the point, I just listened while he voiced his displeasure. He never once yelled—but sometimes I felt that his comments wouldn't have cut so deep if they weren't done with such outward calm and logic. My deep and emotional feelings about the Vietnam War made this a difficult and awkward chapter in my relationship with Coach. After all, he was the one who'd decide if I was ever going to get any meaningful playing time, yet every time I turned around we seemed to be on opposite sides of a controversy. It only served to push us ever further apart.

With my disappointing sophomore year behind me, did I learn my lesson, play hard, and keep my opinions to myself? No such luck. In hindsight, I can see I was still acting out my one-sided father-son fantasy with Coach, but at the time I was convinced I was doing what was right. As a result, as I entered my junior year, Coach and I quickly clashed over his requirement that we all get haircuts that made us stick out on campus like a sore thumb. At a time when long hair and sideburns were the norm for almost everyone but the ROTC, Bruin basketballers were required to look clean-cut and presentable. This policy was uniformly enforced, and every year a couple of players would challenge Coach at the start of practice. But whether the disgruntled player was a little-used reserve like myself, or an All-American like Sidney Wicks or Bill Walton, this "showdown" between Coach and player always ended in the campus barbershop. Coach's rationale for the haircuts was that we were "representatives" of the University of California at Los Angeles, and therefore we had a responsibility to properly present the image of the school to the world at large. No one liked getting their hair cut, but at least he appeared to have a defensible rationale for the policy. But looking around campus, we could see we were representative of no one attending classes. Sitting in a statistics class during my junior year while we were discussing sampling techniques, I had another great idea for how to sway Coach's opinion: I would spend a few hours taking a statistical sample of university students, and then present Coach with a truly accurate picture of the student body we were representing. I figured if I could appeal to Coach's sense of fairness and reason, he would certainly come around. (Well, to be truly candid, I suspect I knew I would make him angry again.)

I figured I couldn't create a scientifically random statistical sample of the UCLA undergraduate population, so I decided to give Coach every benefit of the doubt: I went up to the Math-Sciences quad, where all the conservative geeks with pocket protectors hung out. I charted over one thousand male students as they passed my observation post. Not surprisingly, what became clear was that the clean-cut basketball team was far from representative of the long-haired student population. Once again, oblivious to the predictable sour reaction from Coach, I blithely dropped by his office to discuss how many players on the team should be *required* to have long hair and beards. At the very least, I thought Coach would appreciate the academic rigor and application of learning that I demonstrated in my quasi-scientific study. Maybe he'd even get a chuckle out of it before he turned me down. But Coach saw no humor in my findings, only an irritating challenge to his authority that he clearly did not appreciate. I was turning out to be a real pest.

Mixed in with all the conflict and heartbreak, there

were many fun and memorable moments. I distinctly remember an oddly euphoric sense of invincibility that
reached its zenith in a game in Corvallis against a fine
Ralph Miller–coached Oregon State team. Not to dispar-
age the social scene in Corvallis, but people had been
camping out in the rain for days outside the arena waiting
for our big game. We had barely squeaked past the University of Oregon just a couple nights before, and the
local fans were smelling upset. The crowd was in an absolute frenzy. My role on the team was limited, but I did
have a good hand at providing comic relief, and as we
were about to come out of the tunnel and into the loud
and hostile arena, I let out my best imitation of a ridiculous cartoon character named "Superchicken." Why, I
have no idea. At every road game, when the hated Bruins
ran out of the tunnel and onto the floor, we were greeted
by a wall of boos that almost sucked the air right out of
the gym. The fact that everyone on the team was laughing at my stupid "Superchicken" imitation only served to
enrage the beast. I'm sure these fans thought we were
laughing at them, and the boos got even louder.

As the evening progressed, Oregon State played one of
the best games I had seen a UCLA opponent play in ages.
Led by an outstanding All-Conference guard named Freddie Boyd, who scored 37 points, the Beavers had the lead
with a little more than a minute to play. Timeout was
called, and as the UCLA starters came back to the bench it
seemed a good time for me to let out a real Superchicken
cheer. But why was I cheering, and why were the guys
laughing? I can only speculate, but I think we just *knew*
that somehow this tough opponent was going to give us

the game. Down by a point, a hostile gym, a well-coached opponent with the lead . . . and we were laughing. Sure enough, when play resumed, the reliable Freddie Boyd made his first and only mistake of the game, as under minimal pressure from Kenny Booker he dribbled the ball off his foot and out of bounds. Sidney Wicks dribbled down the clock until only a few seconds remained, faked his slower opponent out of his shoes, and knocked down an 18-foot jump shot for the win. Believe me, we were laughing and screaming as we ran off the floor in front of a stunned group of Beaver boosters. "SUPERCHICKEN!!!" That was really fun.

Though Coach was the first to admit he was no strategic genius, he did occasionally do things that the bench players could only marvel at. While the fans in the stands would comment on Coach Wooden's distinguished demeanor, up close he showed a tougher, more competitive side of his character. Sometimes Coach Wooden's bench jockeying did more to hold down a talented opposing player than the man assigned to guard him. We were playing the University of California at Berkeley in their incredibly noisy cracker box gymnasium. Cal had perhaps the most talent in the conference, but teamwork was not their strong point. Their leading scorer was a powerful 6'5" forward named Jackie Ridgle, who was from a small town in the Deep South. Jackie was a natural scorer, and was averaging well over 20 points a game. We were worried that he might get hot and go for well over his average. But ten minutes into the game, Jackie was not getting many touches, and a heckler on the Bruin bench was giving it to him relentlessly, asking him how he was going to keep his scoring average up if his teammates never gave him the ball. Finally, Jackie looked over to see who was on his case—and he was stunned to see that the guy who was on him was none other than the legendary John Wooden. For the rest of that game Jackie Ridgle just never got it going. We might not have been able to hold Jackie down, but our coach sure got him out of his game.

Near the end of my junior year, we were playing Long Beach State in the NCAA regional finals in Utah. Long Beach State had an excellent team, and that year's UCLA team had the habit of making every game a close one. Oftentimes it seemed as if the team would play lackluster, individualistic basketball for about thirty-five minutes, and then get together for five minutes of team-oriented devastation to save the day. But this particular game against Long Beach State, the starting five was really playing poorly. Now, Coach Wooden always had a hard time understanding the "extracurricular" interests of his young players, but this team had several individuals who partied every bit as hard as they played. One player in particular used to return from every road trip to be greeted by at least three different "girlfriends" who all thought they were his one and only. As the season wore on, it was clear that this particular group of players was unlikely to ever adopt Coach Wooden's views on saving your energy just for the game.

As the second half of this Long Beach State game wore on, it was starting to look like curtains for the Bruins. Long Beach was killing us, and the usual competitive fire that defined the Bruins seemed to be completely lacking. With about seven minutes to play, a timeout was called, and the starters shuffled over to the bench. What then took place left everyone temporarily speechless: Coach Wooden looked his players in the eye, and then accused them all of being a bunch of "All-American blankety-blanks." He didn't actually say "blankety-blanks"; he used a far more accurate term to describe their social proclivities, one that seemed *totally* out of character for Coach. Had he completely lost it? We didn't have time to find out, as he then turned his back and walked away. We were amazed, stunned, surprised . . . and just a little bit amused. Denny Crum realized that time was ticking down, so he jumped in the huddle, got everyone to focus, and talked about the need to hit the boards and get back on defense. As the Bruins ran back out on the floor, the reserves sat back down on the bench not knowing if Coach Wooden had lost it, or if he was the craftiest coach we ever saw. The next six minutes were amazing, as we chipped away at the Long Beach lead. But even with this tremendous effort, Long Beach had the ball and the lead with a little over a minute to go. With no shot clock at that time, all Long Beach had to do was run out the clock and they would be off to Houston's Astrodome for the Final Four. But luck, as usual, was on our side: A Long Beach player took an incredibly ill-advised shot from the deep corner, missed, and the rest was history. As we ran off the floor on the way to the Final Four, we all were chuckling about Coach "losing it" in the huddle.

Another episode that really sticks out in my mind took place midway through my final season at UCLA. This was Bill Walton's first year of varsity basketball, and I'd made sufficient peace with my role that I could enjoy having a seat on the bench to watch this magnificently talented team destroy one opponent after another. We were in Pullman, Washington, for a game with the outclassed Washington State Cougars. Coach did not have a lot of rules, but he was a real stickler for punctuality. As a veteran benchwarmer, I had few rules myself—and the most important rule was to *never* break a team rule unless accompanied by an All-American. Up to some sort of mischief, Bill Walton and I were about ten minutes late to a pregame meal, which would have been a seriously bad move by me had I not been in the company of the finest college center I ever saw. Not wanting to call too much attention to ourselves, Bill and I feigned an air of nonchalance as we strolled into the dining room. We quickly scanned the long table, looking for a seat. Walton, an incredibly quick big man, noticed that only two seats were left, and one was right next to Coach Wooden. So Bill hustled to the seat at the far end of the table, leaving yours truly to sit with Coach. I was prepared for the worst.

Much to my surprise, Coach said nothing about my late arrival. I think he was just thrilled that Walton was okay, and we started to eat our meal. I was seated between Coach and our backup center, who happened to be a likable, sweet, 6'11" kid from the Netherlands named Swen Nater. Swen actually went on to have a very long and productive NBA career, but at that point he was getting no more playing time than I was. He was also pretty gullible, and Coach got on a roll. He spent the next thirty minutes planning a totally fictitious snipe hunt with Swen and me for later that evening. At first, I was egging Coach on, because it seemed like any moment he was going to let Swen off the hook. I was sure that Swen would realize

Coach was pulling his leg when he suggested we meet in the parking lot of the hotel around 2:00 A.M. to go find some "snipe." But Swen was eagerly compiling his list of snipe-hunting essentials: flashlight, pillowcase, and so on. It took all my self-restraint to keep from falling out of my chair. We laughed through the entire meal. When the meal ended, Coach got up, gave me a wink, and walked away. It is important to mention here that Swen was built like Mr. America and weighed about 270 pounds. I thought about Swen standing in the parking lot at 2:00 A.M., and I decided I'd better let Swen in on the joke. No doubt Coach had been the ringleader, but I knew that Swen would have taken it out on me, not him, the next day. Sadly, it was the sort of fun moment that was pretty rare for my mentor and me. And I should note that Bill and I suffered absolutely no consequences for our tardiness. Still, I had no interest in testing Coach on this point again; in three years of varsity basketball, this was the only time I was ever late for anything.

Incredibly, I was always certain that some player would go down with an injury and I would finally get my chance to play. Over time, I think Coach learned to tolerate my idiosyncrasies, and the team continued to win games and championships. In truth, practice was always a joy, and I still loved to play basketball. But as the sand ran out of the hourglass, it became clear that my time at UCLA was going to be distinguished by its lack of highlights. By the time my senior year ended with a third national title, I was really ready to leave my disappointment behind and move on with my life.

Many years after I graduated I played in a business golf game with an old Bruin fan who remembered me from those championship years. He told the other guys in our foursome that I used to be known in Westwood as "the man who starts five thousand cars," because "when he went in the game everyone left." I laughed at his joke, but the truth is that fact still hurt decades later. But how could I tell Coach he needed to play me more when the team was in the middle of the greatest winning streak in the history of sports? By the time I graduated, I had become one of only thirteen men in NCAA history who had played (in my case not much) on three NCAA championship basketball teams. The dream I had as a youngster had come true, but my role was that of a stand-in; the spotlight and stardom belonged to my talented teammates. With my confidence shaken and the future unclear, it was time to put my childhood plans behind me and venture out into the real world.

After college I hooked up with a team in the Israeli professional league for a year, and then spent four years coaching at a local community college. While I was coaching, I would stop in to see Coach Wooden on occasion in the hopes that he might be able to find me a better coaching job. But our conversations were short and somewhat uncomfortable, and no job ever materialized. Going to ball games at Pauley now felt so uncomfortable that I simply stopped going completely. With a push from Gary Cunningham, who by then was the head coach at UCLA and very unhappy with the endless tension and pressure, I got out of coaching basketball. My wife and I were expecting our first child, and it just seemed like it was time to grow up. Coach Wooden, basketball, and UCLA were a part of my past I was eager to leave behind.

• • •

I GOT MY FIRST JOB in the entertainment industry in my late twenties, and I was lucky enough to work for many smart and interesting people. After supervising over eighty hours of movies and miniseries at Columbia Television, I formed my own production company and produced a wonderful Disney-style family movie that was shot on location in Ireland. This movie gave me my first insight into how much I needed to reframe my entire UCLA basketball experience. The picture was called *Three Wishes for Jamie,* and it told the story of a young Irish lad who was granted three wishes by a magical queen. He wished for the chance to travel, to marry the girl of his dreams, and for a fine son who spoke Gaelic. Jamie achieved his first two dreams, but his wife was unable to conceive, and when they finally adopted a child, he was mute. The man became depressed, and his life started to fall apart. In a dramatic final scene, the boy finally speaks, leading the man to realize that he actually had been granted his three wishes.

The picture never got much play, probably because we never found a great young lead actor for the role of Jamie. If we had cast the unknown I wanted, it would have been a much-remembered movie—but my English partners hesitated at casting the totally inexperienced John F. Kennedy, Jr., in the lead. After all, JFK Jr. was playing the fourth lead in an off-Broadway play, so how good could he be? Sadly, we will never know.

I spent over a year developing the script, going to England and Ireland to shoot, and then months of postproduction in England to finish the movie. And it wasn't until we had a rough-cut screening in England that I realized the movie wasn't just about some Irish kid with a dream, it was also about me. I had grown up in Westwood, fantasized about the improbable chance to someday play for the famous Bruins, and then went to UCLA, won three NCAA titles, and was unhappy because I didn't play as much as I wanted. My life and the movie both had three wishes at the heart of their plots. I recognized this to be a sign that I should embrace my Bruin years as a triumph, but it was years before I would really be ready to do so.

After my producing experience in England, I started a television production arm for a major theatrical film producer and made three more television motion pictures. That job led me to my biggest break in the business when I was hired by the CBS network to run their in-house production company. The opportunity was as big as the challenge. With a small staff and a limited budget, we helped create such hit television shows as *Touched by an Angel; Dr. Quinn, Medicine Woman; Walker, Texas Ranger; Dave's World; Caroline in the City;* and *Rescue 911.* At a time when family-oriented programming was no longer in vogue, as president of CBS Productions I played a central role in reintroducing family-oriented hit shows to network TV. The programs that CBS Productions did under my guidance are still seen both in the U.S. and all around the world. When my CBS job ended abruptly, which is common in the entertainment business, I had a nice long paid vacation to contemplate where I was going and how I was going to get there.

My success in the television business was sort of hard to figure. I worked hard, and I was fairly articulate, but I wasn't very corporate, didn't socialize much, and preferred to be with my family. Though it is possible to succeed in show business just because you are devastatingly good-looking, one look at the jacket of this book makes it clear that my looks were not behind my success. But I instinctively understood that I had a gift: I was good at organizing and managing people engaged in a volatile, creative process, and getting them to reach their maximum potential. Creating television shows involves so many egos, so many opinions, so little money, and so little time to get it right, that every show that works is a miracle. A hit television show takes talent, collaboration, and hard work. It just wasn't clear to me exactly how and where I had developed this special ability to manage such an inherently unruly process.

I really was curious where this special management talent I had was nurtured and developed. One of the benefits of taking some time off for introspection is that you finally have a chance to look at your life without ten people standing at the door to your office waiting for an answer. I knew that if I focused enough attention on my past, the truth would eventually come to me.

I was on a golf course when I had my epiphany. Standing over an impossible 210-yard 2-iron shot, my playing partner told me, "You're hurrying; slow down and get your balance." It was as if Coach Wooden was being channeled through my friend. I felt a little bit like Luke Skywalker hearing the sage voice of Obi-Wan Kenobi. My friend had no inkling that his advice was a simple paraphrase of everything Coach had taught us. Sometimes, but not very often, you feel a certain stillness before you swing the club because you just *know* that the shot will be perfect. This was one of those times. When I nailed that shot to within a couple of feet of the hole for a birdie, I knew I had just experienced something that was about more than just a good golf shot. The strength and clarity of that inner voice was so powerful.

From basketball, to golf, to business, I realized that Coach Wooden had actually mentored my entire professional life, and was directly responsible for all my success. What a shock! I had to talk to Coach and share this breakthrough with him.

Unfortunately, I wasn't sure if Coach would even want to talk to me.

I had not really spoken to Coach in almost ten years. I usually only thought about him when I would run into some other former player and we would tell stories about the wild times, the close games, and our shared discomfort with our relationship with Coach. But now I felt that I had to talk with him and share my revelation.

In my business life, I've often had to make unpleasant and potentially explosive calls to network presidents, studio heads, aggressive talent agents, and angry television stars. But I'd never felt this sense of nervousness and vulnerability before placing any of these calls. This wasn't a call to tell someone their show was canceled or their raise denied; I was just calling to express my appreciation to my old coach. Something was pushing me to call, but just as fervently my inner voice was suggesting that perhaps I ought to forget it. Would he pick up the phone? Would he return my call? Heck, Coach was in his late eighties— would he even remember me? I had a whole laundry list of reasons not to call. *He's probably too busy. It would be a terrible imposition on him. He probably just wants to be left alone.* In spite of all these excuses, I knew this was one call I had to make.

Before we dive back into the abyss of conflict that characterized my memories of Coach Wooden, it is important for you to have a clear picture (or at least my clear picture) of this seemingly simple man who many have made out to be almost saintly. John Wooden is not a saint. He is exceedingly smart, well read, and somewhat shy. He loves his family as fully and as deeply as anyone I have ever known, has a deep belief and abiding faith in God, and has an unending admiration for Abraham Lincoln and Mother Teresa. He genuinely cared that his players get an education, which he considered much more important than playing basketball. Everyone calls him Coach, but he was first and foremost *a teacher.* Though retired from coaching for many years now, teaching is so deeply ingrained in his nature that every conversation contains a lesson or quote that enlightens and informs.

It is also true that this outwardly gentle and soft-spoken man might just be the toughest man I ever met. I am sure that many of his former players would concur. No matter how many times this guy got knocked down in his athletic days, there was simply no doubt he was getting back up. He was a tough taskmaster in practice, demanding full attention and effort at all times. When you spend enough time around him, you find he has a biting sense of humor that can be tinged with sarcasm. While many of Coach's staunchest admirers make a big deal out of the fact that he never swears, and it's true that Coach never uses profanity, it is simply ridiculous to say he never swears. Any player who screwed up in practice and was on the receiving end of

Coach's wrath when he would angrily blow his whistle and yell, "Goodness gracious, sakes alive!" knew that he had been "properly" cussed out. John Wooden knew how to swear without using profanity.

This is the man I was going to seek out after almost thirty years, perhaps reopening those old wounds, so I could tell him that I owed everything I now had to his inspired teachings. I felt like I was eating a whole flock of crows—or maybe snipe—but it was something that I simply had to do. I looked through some old appointment books and finally found Coach's phone number. It was really an old number, but I figured if anyone in the entire city of Los Angeles still had the same phone number, it would be Coach Wooden. I mustered up my courage and dialed. I had to suppress a momentary sense of panic that this might be a big mistake—why revisit such long-gone pain? Maybe I should hang up. But I didn't.

After a couple of rings, a machine picked up, which was sort of a relief: At least *he* wasn't on the phone, asking me to remind him who I was—or worse, asking why I would be calling.

The message started to play, "Hello, this is John Wooden. Please speak slowly and distinctly, and leave your name and number after the tone." Hey, this wasn't so hard, I would just leave word, try my best not to expect a call back so my feelings wouldn't be hurt, and move on. The message machine beeped, and I started to speak. "Hi, Coach [I was, of course, speaking slowly and distinctly, since taking orders from Coach seemed natural, even after a quarter of a century], this is Andy Hill." *Wham,* the phone was picked up, and that familiar voice was on the other end. "Andy, where are you, where have you been?"

It was Coach, and his voice was unchanged. It was like being thrown back in time nearly three decades.

But the forbidding Coach of yesteryear wasn't getting on me for a bad crosscourt pass, or annoyed at me for some ill-conceived idea I was asking him to support. He just wanted to know when I was coming to see him. In fact, he really wanted to see me. When Coach suggested that "right now would be fine," it threw me into another moment of panic. Am I really ready for this? Am I better off leaving all this behind me? I had no appointments that day, and could have come over immediately, but I needed some time to think this over. I arranged to come by and see him the next day. I drove to see him with a mixture of positive anticipation and absolute dread. It didn't matter that I hadn't been under his command for almost a quarter of a century; I made sure I arrived on time. I knew better than to be late for an appointment with Coach.

He met me downstairs. I was a bit startled to see how eighty-seven years of life had affected this seemingly indestructible man. In his days as a three-time All-American at Purdue University, John Wooden had been famous for his fearless style of play. Old pictures of him reveal a chiseled, muscular athlete. But nearly sixty-five years later, this reckless abandon had left Coach with hips and knees that gave him a great deal of pain (not that I've ever heard him complain about it). He walked slowly, almost gingerly, to meet me. But the face was familiar, the blue eyes clear, the handshake firm. In an instant we were inside the door of his condo.

To visit Coach in his smallish condominium in Encino is to take a trip back in time. Stuffed full of pictures of his large extended family, it is also filled to overflowing with memorabilia that would blow any college hoops fan's mind. It is also deeply infused with sadness because Coach's beloved wife, Nell, is no longer there to share it with him. I felt surprisingly at ease with him; no longer seated at the end of his bench, hoping desperately that he would put me in the game, I was instead seated comfortably on his couch having a conversation with a much older but most engaging gentleman. My fears and insecurities about how Coach would receive my visit receded and were replaced with a powerful and important sense of reconnection. Though I wasn't too sure of my motivation at the time, I knew I deeply needed to express to him how I now appreciated all he had done for me, and how useful and practical the lessons of UCLA basketball had been for me in the "real world." As much as I had tried to repress my need for approval from Coach, I was aware that somehow his opinions were still terribly important to me.

I sat down and started sharing with him my post-UCLA life story. Coach sat and listened attentively. As I described the relationship between coaching sports and managing a business (my big revelation, as you'll recall) he simply sat there with a beatific smile. Clearly, this big surprise to me was no surprise to him. He nodded and said, "So you did learn something after all." We sat and talked for hours, about life, about family, about values and priorities. My thoughts now mirrored his. I had fought this man, feared him, and at times despised him when I was sitting on the bench as a youngster . . . and now I was just like him. Remarkable! Since that day, I have been back to see Coach many times. I'm still pleasantly surprised that he is always happy to schedule our next get-together. His mind is still sharp and focused. He is nothing less than a national treasure.

My personal journey of reconnection and rediscovery with Coach Wooden has been filled with many warm and wonderful moments. This experience has been one of the great surprises in my life, and it all would have been impossible if I hadn't picked up a phone to say "thanks." If a reader takes nothing else from this book than the inspiration to call an old teacher, mentor, friend, or colleague, then it will be worth the time spent writing it. Everyone has their own list of reasons for not making those calls, and they are invariably as misbegotten as my own list of reasons for not calling Coach.

I see Coach once every month or so. Not surprisingly, he is a man of simple habits. Knowing that Coach's old habits die hard, I make sure that I am *always* on time, even if I have an All-American in tow. I drive into the alley behind his condominium, phone him upstairs, and moments later he comes walking slowly out of the parking garage. It is always hard to see how difficult it is for Coach to get around, since he looks so indestructible in those pictures from his college days when he was known as "The Indiana Rubber Man." His greeting is always short, warm, and pleasant. We then drive over for breakfast at a small coffee shop on Ventura Boulevard. Before walking in, he always wants me to buy him a copy of *The Valley News*, and always tries to force me to take the quarter from him to pay for it. I knew I had made some progress in my relationship with Coach when he finally accepted the paper without trying to pay me back. Then we walk inside the coffee shop, which is an experience in itself. It always reminds me of the bar in *Cheers*, except everyone is over sixty (and they're eating ham and eggs instead of drinking beer). Coach knows every person there, and they all greet him. Coach's son-in-law, Dick, is usually there waiting for us. Family means more to Coach than anything.

Former UCLA assistant coach Gary Cunningham told me he went there once to see Coach and arrived early. He sat at a table, ordered coffee, and then noticed that two elderly women were glaring at him. Soon, Coach arrived, and Gary asked him why these women were staring at him. Coach responded simply, "Well, you *are* sitting at their table." Now you have to believe me, this place is not exactly a four-star restaurant, and the notion that someone had their own personal table is really funny. But Coach wasn't being funny, and they got up and moved tables. It is not a shock that the food is just so-so, but the service is attentive, and Coach is in his element. When the check comes, a brief fight always ensues. His legs may be gone, but his hands are still quick. After breakfast, we go back to his condo for conversation. I learn something every time I see him. When I leave, I always feel somehow calmer and more balanced. He is always teaching. It is in his bones.

So now that I've briefly described my journey of discovery and rediscovery, it is time for me to share my "findings" with you. These principles of coaching that were so unique to John Wooden are all ideas you can incorporate into your own life. I will try to share some examples of how these guidelines applied to the development of the amazing UCLA dynasty, as well as how I used these strategies (albeit unconsciously) to build a hugely successful business myself. But for you to get the most out of what I am about to tell you, there is one more story I have to relate.

Coach's final year at UCLA, though no one knew until the end of the season, was 1975. The Bruins were not expected to win the championship. Coach surprisingly announced his retirement just moments after UCLA defeated Louisville in overtime in the national semifinal game, so Coach's last game had tremendous drama and emotion. In the championship game the Bruins were matched against the favored University of Kentucky team. The Bruins, as they always had under Coach Wooden, only played seven players. Kentucky, which was unusually deep, used ten. As the game progressed, the television commentator kept predicting that Kentucky would eventually wear down the Bruins with their deep bench. This "expert" also spent the whole game asserting that you could not successfully play a man-to-man defense against out-of-bounds plays, as the Bruins were doing against Kentucky. I found this pretty annoying, since UCLA had already won nine national championships employing this strategy. But the Bruins pulled out the victory to send Coach into retirement with his tenth title. After the game, this same commentator, somewhat embarrassed that his prognostication of Bruin defeat had not come to pass, asked Coach what his "secret" was to make his team so well conditioned. Coach smiled and said, "My players *believe* they are in better shape than their opponents." That was it, the whole truth. But this announcer kept asking for clarification: Was it wind sprints, stair climbing, long-distance running? Coach had already told him everything he needed to know, but the analyst was persistent. So Coach just kept his little *Mona Lisa* smile going, knowing that his simple answer had gone right over the announcer's head. Because the fact is, Coach knew that if a player *thought* he was better conditioned than his opponent . . . he *was*.

Keep this story in mind when you read these secrets. Coach's philosophy is based on simplicity. Just like Coach Wooden, these secrets are understandable, accessible, and filled with simple truths. It is no coincidence that the secrets interconnect and overlap in a million different ways. They ultimately form a tight and potent system that has proven its success over long periods of time and despite enormous turnover in key staffing. They also hold the key to unlocking the explosive potential *your* company must exploit to be a dynamic force in the twenty-first century.

While twentieth-century business success was defined by management's ability to streamline production efficiency, as best exemplified by Henry Ford's assembly line, General Patton's relentless war machine, and Vince Lombardi's coolly efficient Green Bay Packers, that paradigm no longer applies to the new century. The companies that can harness creativity and develop new ideas will rule the twenty-first century; computers have made the management of production something best left to machines, and there are few additional efficiencies to be gained on the production side. The challenge for every business is to change the focus of management to reflect the shifting challenges this new century presents. Attempting to manage creativity using the same principles used for managing production efficiency is a recipe for failure.

Managing creativity is a far tougher challenge that requires flexibility, the ability to react and change quickly as market conditions fluctuate, and the skill to empower and nurture fragile egos. Coach Wooden's management concepts are all about creating a structure in which talented, sometimes difficult, creative people are empowered to work together and flourish. Everyone talks about the need to employ "out-of-the-box" thinkers, but managers must realize that most people with the capacity for original thought are not comfortable in a tight and rigid structure. You need to find the balance between creativity and organization. If you accept the fact that the game of basketball is a high-speed contest of discipline, will, talent, organization, and creativity, it will become obvious that no one ever managed this process as successfully and as consistently as John Wooden. Though he coached in the twentieth century, and in some ways seemed old-fashioned even then, John Wooden's organizational approach is actually startlingly futuristic. Far from sacrificing his morals and values to succeed, he incorporated those values into the most triumphant organization of the twentieth century. His methods can unlock the creative power of any group.

So without further ado, here are the secrets of John Wooden's Pyramid of Success. Of course, they aren't really secrets, since every guy who ever played for Coach knows them all by heart. To my Bruin basketball brethren, everything I describe will be so familiar it is almost scary. Integrate these concepts into your own management style and you will succeed beyond your wildest imagination. They are easy to understand, and easy to follow. There is no finer coach, no better teacher, and no more devoted friend and family man than John Wooden. His example is there for us all to follow. The rest is up to you. Be quick, but don't hurry . . . and always be in balance.

II

THE SECRETS

SECRET #1

THE TEAM WITH THE BEST PLAYERS
ALMOST ALWAYS WINS

I TOLD YOU that some of this would sound overly simple. But there are a couple of things to consider here that every manager must be aware of. First of all, identifying talent is a genuine skill. It's true that UCLA had many highly sought-after high school recruits, but there were also plenty of players who weren't on every coach's must have list. Gail Goodrich was considered too small and frail by many college coaches; Keith Erickson was no high school All American; and Fred Slaughter was clearly too small to play major college center at only 6'5". Yet all of these men were outstanding players for Coach Wooden because they fit perfectly within his system. Coach knew what qualities were needed to be successful within the system he ran. Talent can be measured in many ways, and it is vital that you prioritize so you know who will give you the best chance to succeed. *Quickness under control* and *team attitude* were the two attributes that he always put at the top of his shopping list.

Coach was also not afraid to do things his own way. While almost every other coach would sit courtside to scout players, Coach Wooden sat in the corner of the gym at a 45 degree angle. He felt he could judge quickness better from there. It's also true that while most coaches congregate in groups and form a group opinion, Coach Wooden was not interested in fraternizing with the competition; he only wanted his own assistants as company. Quickness was the one ingredient that Coach prized over everything else. When every coach in the country was pursuing Tom McMillen in the early 1970s, Coach Wooden was more interested in a quick, skinny redhead from San Diego named Bill Walton. McMillen went on to have a nice career at Maryland despite never playing in the NCAA tournament, and he eventually went on to the NBA before becoming a United States congressman. But Walton went on to become one of the greatest players of all time, and a cornerstone in the longest winning streak in college history.

Coach also believed strongly in references, not just from a high school player's coach, but also from opposing high school coaches. In fact, he recently told me that he would query four or five opposing coaches about every player he recruited at UCLA. He believed this was far more important than even seeing the player in person. But he maintained total confidentiality about this referral system, which is how he was able to get honest opinions. High school coaches knew that they could share their assessments with him honestly and not get burned by being cited as the reason UCLA wasn't recruiting a certain player. He not only wanted to know about their playing skills, but about their personal character, temperament, and ability to withstand pressure and adversity. Though he rarely visited players in their homes, on one of these visits to see a top high school star, he actually decided not to offer the boy a scholarship because he felt the young man was rude to his mother. Coach was happy to add that this fine player had gone to another school in the conference and played well against UCLA for three years, "But he never did beat us!" With Coach, character really did count

Quickness was the primary physical characteristic he sought, but naturally, he was looking for a combination of quickness and height. Realistically, that was a tough commodity to find in any abundance. But John Wooden knew what he was looking for, wasn't afraid to ask others, and realized that compromise would often be part of the decision-making process. When I asked him who he thought were the best coaches he faced, he said without hesitation, "the ones with the best players." He said it with a smile, but that didn't mean he wasn't serious.

So many top-level managers feel they can make do with mediocre employees as long as they ride them hard. What I learned from Coach is that you must have top-notch talent to succeed. Coach also used a number of interesting strategies to evaluate talent once practices began. In addition to giving his assistant coaches the opportunity to rank the players according to their own sense of where each player stood on the team, Coach also gave the players a rating form to fill out at the beginning of the season. Naturally, Coach eventually took all this input and made these decisions on his own, but giving everyone the sense of having a voice was a powerful tool. Coach would also occasionally "disappear" during practice. In fact, he never left the building; he would go high up into the dark recesses of Pauley Pavilion, where he could watch practice from a different angle and get a better sense of how individuals were fitting into the flow of the game. In short, Coach got as much information from as many different sources as he could—and then he alone made the call.

The ability to evaluate and recruit your "players" is something most managers understand. But there is a secondary corollary to this that is often overlooked, either intentionally or unintentionally. If you have made a mistake and recruited a player who turns out to lack the necessary skills, you have to correct your mistake. There were many high school All-Americans who came to Westwood hoping to play for the Bruins who didn't make the grade. All Coach ever promised was a chance to play, after that it was up to you to perform or get cut. Some players with extraordinary raw talent came to Westwood hoping to be All-Americans, only to find that they couldn't even make the team.

Sometimes you hire people thinking they're talented, only to find out in short order that your judgment was flawed. This happens to everyone. The hard thing is admitting you were wrong and taking action. This means that you have to let people go who can't cut it, and no one likes to fire people. The inability to face up to your mistakes and rectify them is the Achilles' heel of many managers. Firing people is one of the most unpleasant tasks that any manager has to face, but if you aren't prepared to take on the tough tasks, you shouldn't be a manager. The good manager has no choice but to cut people from the squad if they just can't play. You cannot expect to encourage teamwork in an organization where weak performers are allowed to keep their jobs.

One of the first movies I produced was a forgettable television film for ABC called *Ladykillers*. Not exactly the sort of picture you hope to be remembered for, but I did learn a valuable lesson that relates to firing people. Our production designer was supposedly hard at work on plans for the sets he intended to build, and I was looking forward to going over the plans with him before he started construction. Imagine my surprise when he walked in my office and asked me to go over to the sound-stage to look at the sets he had already built. When I asked him why he hadn't shown me the plans, he claimed to have misunderstood my directions. "Besides," he said, "you're gonna love these sets!" I felt like blasting him on the spot, but I held my tongue with the hope that he was right and I was indeed going to love the sets. But when I saw what had been built, I was very unhappy. When I came back to my office, the director came in to see me. One look at my face and he could tell I was upset. When I described what had happened, he immediately said we should fire the production designer and get a new one. I made a couple of weak excuses as to why we shouldn't act so precipitously, but the fact is I just didn't want to go through the unpleasantness of sending this production designer home. The director then explained that while it was fine that I did not want to fire this man, my job *demanded* that I do it. Being the boss is not always doing what you want. I went to see the designer, fired him, and hired a new designer the next day. The sets were built on time and on budget—and the rest of the crew knew that *this* producer was serious about following orders.

Finding the right talent can truly be the difference between huge success and total failure. A perfect example of that happened when we received an order to begin to produce the series based on a pilot called *Touched by an Angel*. The writer-producer who created the show was truly talented, and had done some great work on previous series. But in the process of doing the pilot, it became obvious that he was still struggling with his own belief in a higher power, and would have a very tough time doing a weekly show that focused on faith. The early predictions for the program were so negative that many people felt it would be yanked off the schedule after only one or two episodes had aired. Yet this show was his baby, and replacing him seemed like a heartless act. At the same time, we knew that a woman who had worked with CBS Productions on some other programs was a perfect fit for *Touched by an Angel*. Martha Williamson had a deep personal belief, a wonderful sense of humor, and a boundless imagination. After much soul searching, we decided to bring Martha in as the new writer-producer. It was painful for all involved. In hindsight, this was probably the best decision any of us ever made, since the program has now run for many years and is a cornerstone of the CBS schedule. I should also point out that the creator of the program retained a healthy profit participation in the series, and ended up making a lot of money. So, fortunately, this worked out for everyone. But being the boss sometimes calls for decisions that may seem heartless or unfeeling. Never forget that without the right players on your team, your chances of winning at anything are extremely slim. The leader who recognizes great talent and does not tolerate poor personnel will always succeed.

SECRET #2

BE QUICK—BUT DON'T HURRY!

"**B**E QUICK—BUT DON'T HURRY!** is a phrase that every Bruin player heard constantly. Over and over, day after day, Coach would briefly stop practice, and in sharp, staccato tones, with just a hint of an Indiana twang, snap out, "Be quick—but don't hurry!" It was Coach's mantra. Oftentimes, Coach would crouch down in a defensive stance and move his hands like a lightning-fast magician as he repeated this saying. At times it almost became a joke, but after a while, you began to understand exactly what he meant. Life, like basketball, must be played fast—but *never* out of control. Coach says, "If you hurry, you're more likely to make mistakes; but if you're not quick, you won't get things done. It's like a surgeon who comes upon things that are unexpected. If he isn't capable of responding quickly he may lose a patient. If an attorney isn't a quick thinker, he could lose a case." It's hard to argue with that statement.

Coach's first real exposure to the value of quickness came from his early friendship with legendary Notre Dame football coach Frank Leahy. Leahy took a liking to the young John Wooden when Coach was teaching at

South Bend High School, and Leahy gave him an open invitation to attend Notre Dame football practices. The quickness with which the Notre Dame players shifted from one drill to another as soon as the whistle blew and an order was barked out made a strong impression on Wooden. He also observed that these great Notre Dame teams were actually lighter than most of their opponents, but prevailed because of their superior quickness, agility, and precision. Leahy's practices were short and efficient, and Wooden's practices followed the same pattern. It is interesting that Notre Dame football had a profound impact on the future success of the UCLA basketball program; Frank Leahy's lessons stayed with Coach Wooden for a lifetime.

Coach's emphasis on quickness revealed itself in many ways. When the UCLA team started to use the full-court press in the early 1960s, this tactic was almost non-existent in college basketball. John Wooden's Bruins were undersized but remarkably quick athletes. Blessed with fast feet as well as fast minds, their relentless pressure in the full-court press set them apart from the rest of the competition and brought Coach Wooden his first NCAA championship team in 1964. So it was not surprising to see coaches all over America copying the Bruins—and almost none of them really understood the purpose of the press. Despite what most other coaches assumed was true, the Bruin press was really not designed to *steal* the basketball. The press was installed to make the other team play at a faster tempo. What Coach knew, because he spent so much time teaching his players to resist the temptation, was that most young players would play *too fast* if given the chance.

Remember that all these players were just college kids; every one of them had been high school stars who were faster and more talented than their opponents. They all thought themselves capable of making any play, converting any shot, and stealing any pass. It was just not in their nature to ever think of slowing down; they all wanted to go faster and faster, which was why the job of slowing them down was such a priority for Coach. He devoted more teaching to this one point than to any other.

Coach Wooden's genius was in helping his players find and maintain that razor's edge between quickness and hurrying. Some players, like Jamaal (Keith) Wilkes, seemed to naturally play at that perfect pitch. Others spent years in search of it. Coach was a great believer in quickness, which he explained by telling me, "When you learn something, you must be quick in implementing it. It's like driving the freeway. You may know what to do, but if you don't do it *quickly,* you may not be around very long." But when I asked Coach to define the difference between *quickness* and *hurrying,* he surprised me by saying, "Some may not see the difference, but I do—I just cannot explain it." Now that's weird to hear from Coach, who never seemed at a loss to explain almost anything. But he was now sounding cryptic, almost like Yoda. Even at 90, Coach is still full of surprises.

I have met many people in my years in communications, but no one has nearly as many sayings, quotations, and homilies as Coach Wooden. He can tell you endless stories about the life of Abraham Lincoln; extol the virtues of his personal hero, Mother Teresa; recite poems for hours; and deliver snappy sayings that you've heard him say before but can't ever quite remember. But none of us could ever forget "Be quick—but don't hurry!"

Of course, there are many facets that define the edge of quickness. Coach summarizes them as follows: "If you don't have physical balance, you cannot be quick. To have physical balance, it must be preceded by mental balance and emotional balance. If you don't have those, you will be hurrying. Then you will have activity without achievement." *Activity without achievement* seems an excellent way to describe an awful lot of the basketball you see today.

Coach even followed this concept when he ate dinner, a trait I remember seeing the first time I met him as a seventeen-year-old high school senior. Jerry Norman, the top UCLA assistant at that time, had scouted a few of my high school games, and he invited me to come up and meet Coach Wooden at the training table. I was so awestruck I was afraid I would barely be able to speak. So when I sat down between Coach Wooden and his 7'1" All-American center Kareem Abdul-Jabbar, I simply hoped to remember my manners and not embarrass myself. So we sat down, started to chat, and then I noticed that Coach had quickly cut up his entire steak. As I tried to sound composed and intelligent, Coach wolfed down that steak in short order. He never seemed to rush, but that steak was gone in a flash. No wasted motion, no wasted time. It seemed like days before I was finished with my meal. It was my first up-close exposure to "Be quick—but don't hurry!"

The famous UCLA full-court press really grew out of a keen understanding of the need to "Be quick—but don't hurry!" We have all heard expressions like "He who hesitates is lost," but Coach knew instinctively that "Speed kills" was equally true. Coach wanted his players to operate at that edge just before it was no longer possible to be in balance, properly assess their options, and react appropriately. There was no situation we could think of where Coach might not interject his favorite saying. It was so ingrained, I'm sure it was already in our heads before he could even get the words out. Though quickness was the hallmark of UCLA teams, the fact that they played under control was equally important. A reporter, knowing of his passion for quickness, once asked Coach why a certain extremely quick player was not getting more court time. Coach acknowledged that the youngster was quick, but then added, "He hasn't gotten anything done yet . . . but he sure is quick."

One way that Coach instilled this concept in everyone was by integrating it into everything we did. It even had an impact on what happened before the game started. When UCLA played on the road we would usually come out for warmups before our opponents. When the Bruins were in town, students from the opposing school often camped out for days to get the chance to sit up close and jeer the champion Bruins. Typically, the hostile arena would burst into deafening boos as soon as we came on the court. After a few minutes of running layup drills, the din would still be at a fever pitch. Then something really strange would happen: We would spend a few minutes running through the famous UCLA high-post offense. This could have looked pretty ridiculous (after all, no one was playing defense), were it not for the speed, timing, and crispness that was a trademark of Wooden's teams.

Slowly, the booing and catcalls would die down, to be

replaced by an odd (or awed) silence as the capacity crowd watched this embodiment of "Be quick—but don't hurry!" The sound of sneakers squeaking on hardwood and crisp passes slapping the palm of the outside hand of the receiver was the only sound in the arena. The crowd sat hushed as the Bruins gave a high-speed rendition of our most basic principle. What a remarkable sensation it is to experience a boisterous, obnoxious, rowdy group of fans turning their collective attention toward a carefully choreographed, high-speed dance of basketball poetry. They weren't sure *why* this was special, but they did know they were seeing something worth watching.

Be quick—but don't hurry! also applies to our expectations of anything we can hope to accomplish, and how quickly we can expect to get there. Impatience and unrealistic goals will sabotage a talented group of individuals in any workplace. Set your sights too high, and expect immediate attainment of your goals, and invariably you will never reach your destination. It is vital to focus on things that you can actually control, like your own effort, as opposed to external goals over which you have no control.

Executives and leaders in every business should strive for quickness in their work. Nothing holds back progress and deflates morale more than the slow and never-ending "maybe." Commit to answers quickly and your staff will feel empowered to move forward. Affirmative responses always boost morale, but even if you decide *not* to move forward, your team will understand they need to develop a new strategy, and they will keep moving forward. Mistakes are inevitable, but mistakes made because you cannot commit to a path of action are unforgivable. Of course, part of this requires that you be equally quick to admit that you have made a mistake, and then you must work as quickly as possible to rectify the problem.

In my many years in the television business, one of the best decisions I made was the commitment to *quickly* respond to creative materials. A story outline, a first-draft screenplay, or a rough cut of an episode or movie always received a very fast response. Someone early in my career explained to me a very simple truth: If you wait three weeks to respond to everything, at the end of the year you will still have to read the same number of scripts, you will just always take a longer time to respond. If you can't quite follow that one, read it again. What is important to realize is that when a creative person has handed their work to you, they are on pins and needles until they hear if you like what they've done. Most creative people are a little neurotic to start with, so I figured that my behavior shouldn't add to their normal level of anxiety. I therefore incorporated the need for quickness into all of my creative interactions. But I also made sure that before every creative meeting, I had a separate creative meeting with my development team to discuss *their* reactions to the script. The time to do that is before meeting the writer, not during that meeting. So while we were quick, we refused to hurry. Sound and powerful advice from Coach.

Particularly today, in this rapidly changing business environment where the rules of the Internet are reinvented almost monthly, there is never enough time to be sure . . . and if you are sure, you are probably already too late. The need to follow Coach's exhortation to quickness is greater than ever. Never forget that Coach repeated his mantra many times every day, because he knew how central it was to the team's success. But he also knew that this simple lesson was extremely hard to put into action. Most people are naturally hesitant, and the Wooden approach was to remove all hesitation from the game. If you can remove hesitation from *your* game, you'll be well on your way to being a better leader, and your organization will run more efficiently.

We all know executives and managers who just can't seem to make a decision. Give me more data, they demand. Let's have more meetings, draft more reports, get more opinions. They always want to spend more time . . . they need to think about it. It never occurs to them that their indecision is nothing more than an inability to act. Learn to trust your instincts. When you do have a sense of what to do, don't be afraid to pull the trigger! Business, like basketball, is a game that is controlled by the quick and the nimble!

SECRET #3

FOCUS ON EFFORT, NOT WINNING

I KNOW it's hard to believe, but Coach never emphasized winning. What he talked about was the commitment to playing your hardest. *Don't permit fear of failure to prevent effort. We are all imperfect and will fail on occasion, but fear of failure is the greatest failure of all.* If you gave it your best and lost, that was fine. In fact, that was better than winning with a mediocre effort.

It's not that Coach didn't care about winning. I don't think I've ever met a more competitive man in my life. But he was smart enough to know that people focus too much on the score and tighten up. Of course, when you're the top-rated team in the country and Coach gives you the locker room speech about how all he cares about is a good effort, it's hard not to chuckle just a little. After all, the only time the Bruins ever seemed to lose (which was rare) was when the effort just wasn't quite there. On the other hand, Coach gets genuinely annoyed when people talk about giving 110 percent effort, because the goal is ridiculous. Even giving a full 100 percent effort is only approachable, and probably never attainable. But any individual or team that gets close to a full effort will win far more than they lose. Some cynics might point out that it was easy for Coach to focus on effort when he already had all the best players, but Coach was not always blessed with the most talented ballplayers. His focus on effort was the same when his big man was a great player like Bill Walton or Kareem Abdul-Jabbar, a good player like Steve Patterson, or an average player like Doug McIntosh—and he won with all of them, too!

John Wooden's father was a driving force in shaping his views. From an early age, young John was taught: "Don't whine, don't complain, don't make excuses . . . just do the best you can." In Indiana, high school basketball is beyond huge, and the state tournament is the biggest event of the year. In John Wooden's senior year of high school, his team lost the state championship game by a single point. Young John was the only team member who didn't cry after the loss. He was disappointed, but following his father's yardstick of success, he knew he had competed as hard as he could. There is no doubt that valuing effort over winning was something that Coach had integrated into his highly competitive nature at a very early age. His father told him, "Johnny, don't you try to be better than your brothers. But try to be the best you can be. You're gonna be better than some, and there are gonna be some better than you. You've got to accept that. But you should never accept the fact that you didn't make the effort to do the best that you can do." Young Johnny Wooden listened closely to his dad, and passed that lesson on to a lot of other young men.

Coach would even go so far as to say that the general view of winning is not something he necessarily shares. He wanted the victories that most people considered success to simply be the by-product of the effort made to get there. Now you are probably asking, is this guy serious? Absolutely. Coach likes to cite Cervantes, who said, "The journey is better than the inn." He is also fond of quoting Robert Louis Stevenson, who said, "To travel hopefully is a better thing than to arrive." Many of Coach Wooden's philosophies are supported by quotes from famous authors and philosophers, which he can rattle off at the drop of a hat. This next quote is one he first came across when he was teaching high school in South Bend, Indiana, and it rolls off his tongue more than sixty years later like he just memorized it yesterday: "At God's footstool to confess, a poor soul knelt and bowed his head. I failed, he cried. The master said, thou didst thy best . . . that *is* success." He really does judge success by effort and by how close a group comes to realizing their own potential. By this standard, any team has the opportunity to achieve great success.

His most satisfying seasons did not all end with a national title, but many times were the teams that had come closest to achieving their potential whether winning the title or not. More than fifty years after his first season at UCLA in 1948–49, Coach still considers that first squad one of his most satisfying, despite the fact that they did not go on to postseason success. But that team, picked to finish last in the conference, ended up winning 22 games and the conference title, still one of Coach's proudest accomplishments. Winning was a by-product of effort, not an end product.

Coach's genius was in understanding that those who spend all their time talking about winning aren't helping their chances. Every player I've spoken to mentions that removing winning as the focal point reduced the pressure and fear they felt entering a game. Coach also minimized the pressure in the final minutes of the game by insisting that a free throw missed in the first minute was just as important as a free throw missed in the final minute. Once again, this spread responsibility onto every player throughout the entire game, not one individual at the end.

When a leader can consistently and positively reinforce the value of maximum effort, the results are often surprising. One of the truly radical things about the UCLA basketball program was that punishment in the form of wind sprints or running stadium stairs just never happened. Instead of making conditioning a chore, it was totally integrated into all of our drills; staying in shape wasn't treated as a necessary evil, but was naturally achieved as a by-product of effort within our normal drills. Anyone can be in fantastic physical shape; it's just a matter of effort and dedication. And year after year, without punishment or negativity, John Wooden's Bruins were the best-conditioned team in the country.

The key point here is that *effort is internal,* and is completely within your control. Winning is a by-product of effort, but it is subject to external factors and is almost never completely within your control. The referees might make bad calls, the shots may not be falling, your star player may be hurt. In large organizations, it usually takes a concentrated effort from many people to achieve success, but often people get so distracted and sidetracked by what others are doing that they don't concentrate on their own tasks and do their best work. But you can *always* strive to focus on doing your very best, making *that* the goal you're shooting for, whether you're playing basketball or competing in the business world, or simply try-ing to have a good marriage and a close family. As Coach says, "You can fool your boss about your effort, you may be able to fool your wife about your effort, but you can never fool yourself."

Might an organization meet more of its objectives by focusing on effort rather than outcome? Absolutely! Fo-cusing on effort is the way to get the very best out of em-ployees in an organization. Many things happen that are out of any individual's control; employees who are asked to be accountable for a group outcome invariably suc-cumb to the anxiety and pressure that this lack of control creates. But if everyone's effort is continuous and sus-tained, and not concentrated in short bursts, then your employees will grow confident in their ability to work ef-ficiently and consistently. Concentrate on your job, give it maximum effort, and if the rest of the organization is doing the same thing, success is virtually unavoidable.

When I worked on *Touched by an Angel* at CBS, we had to completely rework our first episode and had very little time in which to create a new prototype. Everyone had ideas about how to improve on the original pilot, and many of those ideas were right on target. We were well aware that critics and advertisers were convinced that the program wouldn't last long, and our slim chance for suc-cess seemed to rest entirely on the quality of this one episode. Succeeding might change the future of the net-work and be worth hundreds of millions of dollars; fail-ure would result in substantial financial and emotional losses. Talk about pressure; this was as tough as it gets.

As I've mentioned, we brought in Martha Williamson to write the script. Her first task was to listen to the notes and suggestions of countless executives. They were all smart, and all well meaning, but she was going crazy trying to please all of these people and making sure to address all the notes. Countless people reminded her that without some brilliant revisions we were facing oblivion. But it was also obvious to me that audience reaction is always hard to gauge, and to use Nielsen ratings to measure the success of a writer's revisions was neither fair nor productive. I told Martha that she had to stop trying to please everyone else, and to go off to write a script that would please *her*. Most competitive people are their own toughest critics, and if she could produce a script that she judged as her best effort, then the process would be successful regardless of audience reaction. As Coach would say, winning is the *by-product* of effort. Years later, Martha told me that was a real breakthrough point for her in the evolution of this wonderful show. She wrote for the only audience she could control: herself.

SECRET #4

KEEP IT SIMPLE

T HERE WAS NO simpler program in America than UCLA in its heyday. We had one defense (man-to-man), one out-of-bounds play, a simple high-post offense, and the firm belief that a fifteen-foot bank shot at the end of a fast break was a fine result. Scouting UCLA was a waste of time; our opponents knew what we were going to do—they just couldn't stop it. Coach ran the exact same offense his entire coaching career, which spanned forty years, except for the six years in which he had the two greatest centers of all time. But without Kareem or Bill, the Bruin plays were so familiar that they were run by high school teams all over America. One clear by-product of the simplicity of this system is that it could be run to absolute perfection. In Coach's words, "The more you make things complicated, the more there is to learn. Keep things as simple as you can and you have a chance to do them better. I'd always rather do a few things well." We learned our lessons so well that when I played in an alumni game nearly fifteen years after I graduated, the plays were still completely fresh in my memory!

Coaches all over America would watch UCLA play,

and suggest to their players that the fifteen-foot bank shot was a great way to finish the fast break. But did any of them realize how much time we spent shooting those bank shots? Every day, all year, every year, bank shots took up fifteen to twenty minutes of practice time at UCLA. Not only did we focus on shooting bank shots, we focused extensively on going to the likely rebounding spots in case the shooter missed. So instead of a fast break that featured the risky passes, offensive fouls, and multiple turnovers that can result from taking the ball to the basket, the UCLA fast break was beautifully designed to get us a shot we'd practiced over and over and over. It was also amazing how often the "lucky" Bruins were able to rebound their missed bank shots. Of course, if we had to learn four or five defenses, multiple offenses, and a myriad of out-of-bounds plays, there just wouldn't have been time to perfect this simple play.

Excessive coaching is one of the most common errors that managers make. Meetings that last for hours on end rarely result in a clear and common goal. But the instinct to overcoach is understandable, since it gives managers the false sense that they've done a superb job, and it's up to their underlings now not to let them down. The strong leader who is secure enough to give simple instructions and trust his followers' ability to implement them will almost always come out ahead. There is risk involved in this strategy, because if your team doesn't reach its goal, you may be accused of being overly simplistic. You must be willing to run this risk, since a great leader will always take the blame for his team's shortcomings regardless of the reasons for failure. But some managers always look to divert blame onto others; we've all worked with and for managers like this, and they may succeed for a while, but ultimately their style fails them.

I always felt that if you couldn't give a writer creative notes in an hour or so, you were making the process too complicated. Many television executives would have two-, three-, and even four-hour meetings with writers. I insisted that we keep meetings short, and focus on conceptual issues rather than specific line notes. In fact, one of the best pieces of advice I ever got in guiding the process with creative people is that the truly gifted executives end their sentences with question marks, not exclamation points. Ask a writer what they want a scene to accomplish or a character to be and it challenges them to create an answer; tell them what *you* think it should accomplish, and it constricts that person's creative flow. Your job is to coax the best work out of an individual, not to do it for them. And if the creative person you're working with can't answer your questions in compelling ways, you need to get a new person for the job.

When CBS executives screened the pilot for *Dr. Quinn, Medicine Woman,* a show that had simplicity written all over it, most of them proclaimed it was "like watching paint dry" and that no one would watch it. Where were the chase scenes, the sex scenes, and the fancy visual effects? But we had tremendous belief in the program's simplicity, and felt that it had the potential to be a breakout hit. It took our testing the show with thousands of viewers and hearing their wildly enthusiastic feedback to get CBS to give the country a chance to "watch paint dry" every Saturday night. In fact, when the show was given a Saturday evening time slot, it was assumed by most experts that this was tantamount to a death sentence, since

CBS hadn't had a hit show on Saturday night in over a decade. But the experts were wrong: *Dr. Quinn* went on to win its time period and set off a run of tremendous dominance for CBS on Saturday night. It turned out to be one of the greatest success stories of TV in the 1990s—and it was just a simple show.

There's a funny story about the program that speaks to the need to maintain your belief in simplicity even when others want more flash. *Dr. Quinn* had already debuted to big ratings, but some executives at the network were still certain that we needed more action in the show. We knew that the audience for this program wasn't coming to see action, but were responding to the emotional and poignant personal stories. One executive was convinced that the rugged mountain man character Sully (played by Joe Lando) needed to throw his tomahawk in every episode. What were we to do? After all, it would take a great deal of storytelling time to find a motivation for this type of violent incident every week. Then we hit upon a great idea for how to make sure the tomahawk was thrown in each episode: We filmed Joe Lando throwing it, and put it into the title sequence of the program. That way, I could truthfully answer that the tomahawk was thrown each week—even though he almost never actually threw it in an episode! We kept our simple show simple, and still gave this executive what he asked for.

Perhaps the most crucial benefit of Coach Wooden's simple approach to the game was the confidence and sense of trust that it communicated to our team. With no emphasis on sleight-of-hand maneuvers or trick plays, the players clearly understood that the outcome was dependent on their skills, their effort, and their willingness to work together. This message was never overtly communicated, but it was clearly understood. We knew that our opponents knew exactly what we were going to do, but we also knew that it wouldn't matter. Confidence is an essential ingredient in any competitive environment, since it not only bolsters your chances of winning, but also keeps your organization steady and focused when you're confronted with adversity. Coach Wooden clearly proved that simplicity and success go hand in hand.

SECRET #5

MAKE YOUR "YES" MEAN YES

AMBIGUITY AND lack of clarity are unhelpful to any organization. Intellectually, that's something most managers understand, but far too often a sense of confusion results from unclear signals from the top. Coach Wooden knew that he had to demonstrate the behavior he expected his players to exhibit. Unlike Bobby Knight, who expected complete discipline and self-control from his players while exhibiting none of that discipline and control himself, Coach set the tone for everyone. He expected honesty, responsibility, and directness from others, so he embodied those characteristics himself. One of his favorite expressions was, "Make your 'yes' mean yes, and your 'no' mean no." What could be simpler than that? But in this Clintonian age of parsing sentences, it is often difficult to know what people really mean. John Wooden was not a man who parsed sentences.

In fact, if he wasn't a man who kept his word, John Wooden probably would never have coached at UCLA. While he was coaching at Indiana State in the late 1940s, he was in the running for jobs at the University of Minnesota and UCLA. He preferred Minnesota, and hoped to get the job there; it was a much more prestigious position, since West Coast basketball was not as respected as Big Ten hoops. But he couldn't keep UCLA on the string forever, so Coach gave the Minnesota athletic director a deadline to make him an offer, with the firm hope that the offer would be forthcoming. The deadline passed, and Coach Wooden did not hear from Minnesota. So, true to his word, he called UCLA and accepted their offer. The next day, the Minnesota officials called to offer him the job that he had wanted. It turned out that a snowstorm had knocked out the phone lines, which was why they hadn't reached him the day before. This was completely understandable and certainly constituted extenuating circumstances—but Coach Wooden had given his word to UCLA that he accepted their deal, and the rest is history. His "yes" had meant just that.

In some ways, this expression also stood for the way that Coach stood firm in his decision making. While spots in the starting lineup were wide open at the start of practice, by the end of the preseason Coach had firmly decided who was going to play; the top seven or eight players had been identified, and that was that. While many reserves were frustrated by this rigid system, the guys who were playing benefited greatly from this sense of certainty. No player had to wonder if Coach was going to change his mind on a whim; he had made his decision, and he would stand by it. In my junior year, one of our starting guards, Henry Bibby, struggled through a terrible stretch of games. Any other coach in the country would have started juggling his lineup, but not Coach Wooden, and Henry managed to snap out of his slump and played spectacularly in the NCAA tournament. Once Coach made up his mind, he stood his ground.

I've found this characteristic to be incredibly important when dealing with creative people. Giving clear and firm answers, while not always pleasant, does allow projects to move forward without a lot of wasted time. In order of preference, the best answers are "yes" and "no," with "maybe" in distant third place. But so many managers are afraid of hurting feelings, and feel that "maybe" is less disappointing. Of course, in the short term they're correct, but in the long term they're very wrong. Naturally, this clarity of intent and purpose shows people that you're a person of integrity—and that is a vitally important trait when dealing with creative people. The value of their knowing where you stand, and believing that your word is your bond, far exceeds the temporary inconveniences and setbacks that will inevitably result from telling people where they stand and sticking with your judgment. Remember, Coach Wooden thought that having to turn down the University of Minnesota was a real bad break—but that "bad break" turned out awfully well for all concerned.

SECRET #6

BALANCE IS **EVERYTHING**

HERE'S ANOTHER ONE of Coach's mantras that we used to hear all the time: Your head always has to be at a midpoint between the feet. Over and over, in practice after practice, Coach would blow his whistle and chastise a player for being out of balance. That meant no fall-away jump shots, no leaping-leaners (well, maybe Walt Hazzard got away with a few, but no one else did). On the fast break, the ball handler in the middle *always* stopped at the free throw line—no wild drives, blind passes, or charging fouls in a UCLA fast break! The same was true on defense, where posture, balance, and keeping your hands close to your body were constantly stressed. Blocked shots and steals were fine, so long as the player was in control—but control was paramount. Without balance, there is no control. Coach tried to stress balance in your personal life as well . . . but, well, it was the early 1970s. So while Coach was practicing balance in his own life (he always stressed that his family was far more important to him than anything he did at work), most of us ignored his advice and lived like the crazy college kids we were.

John Wooden did not just talk about the need for balance; everything in his life suggested that he lived those values as well. His love for his wife and family were evident to everyone in the program. It was clear to us that there actually were things in his life more important than the score of a basketball game, and that keeping perspective was crucial to maintaining consistency. Coach also was a man of faith, and though he never tried to influence any of us to share his beliefs, he always made it clear that he believed it was important to have a religious faith in your life. Coach Wooden's ability to mix family, friends, and faith with his job as basketball coach made him a role model we all could look up to. Too often leaders give their team the impression that the next game is somehow a matter of life and death, which of course is never the case. The sense of balance between Coach's personal and professional lives had an overall calming effect on the entire program. Though we only lost three times in the three years I played for Coach, his behavior was always consistent with his philosophy. While he could be stern and express anger, there were never any tantrums, no lockers kicked, no objects thrown. Wins were "pleasing" and losses were "disappointing," and Coach clearly viewed basketball as a part of life, not life itself.

Balance on a basketball team has many facets. Coach summarizes them as follows: "I must have offensive balance, defensive balance, squad balance, emotional balance, mental balance, balance, balance, balance." He feels just as strongly about balance in one's personal life. Keeping perspective on things is a way to keep your balance, and Coach feels it is one of the cornerstones of personal happiness. He might be onto something, because he is one of the happiest people I know.

As much as Coach wanted to win, he never sacrificed family obligations for the sake of the basketball program. In his early days at UCLA, Coach had a run-in with a talented but headstrong star named Eddie Sheldrake. Players got married younger in those days, and Eddie's wife was expecting to deliver their child at a time when the Bruins were scheduled to play a crucial game out of town. Eddie and Coach often did not see eye to eye—but in a surprising twist, it was Coach Wooden who insisted that Eddie miss the trip and be with his wife. Though there are some players today who might insist on being present for the birth of their children, it is hard to imagine any contemporary coach who would *insist* that a key player miss a game so he could be in attendance. And this was in the early 1950s, when men were largely relegated to the waiting room, so Coach Wooden's insistence on Eddie missing the game was even more notable. For those of us lucky enough to have children, we know that being present at the birth of your children is probably life's greatest event. When you're a headstrong kid of twenty-one like Eddie Sheldrake was, that's hard to see, but he was lucky enough to play for a man who knew that no ball game was worth not being with your wife while she gives birth. It's also a clear example of Coach being ahead of his time in his approach to understanding his players' needs.

Balance also manifested itself in the diversity of players in John Wooden's basketball program. Not only was there always a racial balance on the team, but the players came from extremely varied home situations. Keep in mind that balance of this type does not always make for smooth sailing. Coach Wooden's first national championship team in 1963–64 featured a flashy black kid from urban Philadelphia (Walt Hazzard), a middle-class white kid from the San Fernando Valley (Gail Goodrich), a poor black kid from rural South Carolina (Kenny Washington), and a tough, upper-middle-class Jewish kid from Los Angeles who was born in Brooklyn (Jack Hirsch). This group had very little cohesiveness off the court, where their strong personalities often clashed—yet in terms of a group that blended well and competed hard as a team, Coach Wooden feels that this was perhaps the best team he ever coached. Diversity can be a real advantage if it's properly channeled.

I was fortunate enough to balance my professional life with a family and a spiritual life; many people in Hollywood forgo everything for their career. I believe that the balance I had in my personal life led to the success I found in business. Because many people in the entertainment business spend all their time in either Los Angeles or New York, the rest of the country is nothing more than a secondary consideration in their decisions. To those people, a show like *Touched by an Angel* seemed ludicrous. Far from making time for faith and family, they burn the candle at both ends. Concepts like faith in God, belief in your fellow man, and commitment to helping others are totally foreign to their lives and careers. Fortunately, like Coach, I had come to understand the pivotal role that faith and family can play in balancing your life, so when this program about faith came along, I deeply believed that it could be successful. The balance that at times felt like an impediment to success turned out to be the key to success.

Balance in your personal life also lets you keep moving

forward when things aren't necessarily going your way. Haven't you noticed that you can negotiate a better deal when you know that losing the deal isn't the end of the world? Or that you do better in job interviews when you ask as many questions as you're answering? When people perceive that you're on the brink of a total meltdown, they can simply wait you out and watch you fall. But the strength and calm you project when you're truly balanced make you far more powerful than when you come across as about to come unglued. Being in balance also gives you the ability to react and adjust to changes in the marketplace without a lot of wasted motion. When you're out of balance and overcommitted to a particular path, bad things can happen. In this respect, business can be much like a golf swing: When done smoothly and in balance, great things can happen. But squeeze the club, take a huge backswing, and swing your hardest, and the result is almost always bad.

When a manager has true balance, employees know that there is strength and vision at the head of the organization.

SECRET #7

A GOOD LEADER IS FIRST, AND FOREMOST, A TEACHER

COACH OFTEN talked about his days as a high school English teacher. He always had a somewhat scholarly approach to basketball, and he wanted his players to understand *why* they were executing an assignment. He also believed strongly that coaches must set an example and be a role model. One of Coach's favorite expressions is, "No written word, no spoken plea, can teach our youth what they should be. Nor all the books on all the shelves: It's what the teachers are themselves." But being a teacher also meant breaking things down to their basic fundamental components, and then making them second nature by repetition. From tying your shoelaces, to proper technique on a bounce pass, to pointing "man and ball" on defense, Coach was always teaching. To this day he sees himself as more a teacher than a coach. When he talks about his past teams, he's far more likely to talk about "teaching" a team than "coaching" them. An interesting and little known sidebar is that John Wooden did not set out to be a teacher, but he actually wanted to be a civil engineer. Unfortunately (or so he thought at the time), engineering students were forced to attend a mandatory, unpaid summer program while in college, and John Wooden needed a job to make money. Hard to imagine that he might never have taught or coached if not for a summer school requirement for civil engineers!

His approach to coaching very much mirrored the things he learned from years of teaching English. First and foremost, Coach broke down teaching into a set of four core components: demonstration, imitation, correction, and repetition. In his mind, these four principles were the key to effective teaching. He was thrilled to share with me the following poem, which was written by former teammate Swen Nater. Swen played only sparingly in college, yet was a first-round NBA draft choice and went on to a long and successful career in the pros. He is one of many former players who stay in regular contact with Coach Wooden, but maybe the only one who sends poems and recordings of songs he writes and sings. Coach has always loved poetry, and Swen Nater is the poet laureate of UCLA basketball. By the way, before you get the urge to make fun of Swen's poem, keep in mind that Swen is 6'11", weighs 275 pounds, and is still in great shape! Here's Swen's poem, "The Four Laws of Learning":

At the start of all your teaching,
You would show me what to do.
Always leading by example,
DEMONSTRATION of "how to."

Then you'd say, "Why don't you try it.
I have shown you how to be."

IMITATION—I attempted,
As you watched me lovingly.

"Do it this way. Do it that way.
Try it once again like this."
Your CORRECTION drilling habit,
As we watched my skills progress.

With occasional assistance,
You retreated humbly.
You were finished—I had learned it.
REPETITION was the key.

Coach's greatest gift is not *what* he taught us, but the fact that he really taught us how to *learn*. Bill Walton, one of the two greatest centers in the history of college basketball, tells a wonderful story of his life after the NBA that really makes this lesson clear. Bill always set his goals extremely high, and his post-playing aim was to make a career in broadcasting. His ability to speak clearly when he was in college was limited at best; it wasn't until he was in his late twenties that, with the help of the New York–based broadcasting legend Marty Glickman, Bill really taught himself to speak clearly. Glickman gave him a short set of general tips on how to improve his speaking, and then implored Bill to apply the learning techniques he had learned from Coach Wooden. Glickman's tips included slowing your thoughts down and not hurrying, practicing your weaknesses by reading out loud, watching yourself in the mirror, and being unafraid to make mistakes. Sound familiar? Bill integrated these tips into Coach's laws of demonstration, imitation, correction, and repetition. Bill sure learned his lessons well; at times, I think everyone who hears Walton on TV longs for the days when he barely spoke at all. To this day, Coach Wooden always tells Bill that he talks too much.

There are several other teaching principles that Coach integrated into his coaching techniques that can be emulated in any workplace. He believed in ending practice on time, and he always wanted to go out on a fun and positive note. He'd set up either a shooting game or some sort of contest, something that brought us together as a group so we went out on a high note. He emphasizes this point in clinics he gives to young coaches by saying "It's always wise to end practice on a high note. It's good to go home on a high note. Particularly when you are a young coach. When you're older, it doesn't make that big a difference."

Finding ways to end workdays on an up note is a positive challenge for all managers. Coach also found in his teaching days that complicated theories and concepts were best introduced at the beginning of class, before a fatigue factor set in. This was even more evident on the basketball court. This same principle applies whenever you're teaching your group new things, or when you're scheduling important meetings. We've all gone to late-in-the-day sales meetings where the buyer could barely stay focused. Try to set up big meetings for early in the day, before you have to fight fatigue.

Many managers expect their employees to know all the intricacies and nuances of their jobs from the day they start work. This is unrealistic, and often results in hiring mediocre employees whose only real virtue is experience. Be patient, don't assume job skills, offer simple explanations, and insist on repetition so that good habits are ingrained. So many managers fail in their responsibilities because they're afraid to intervene and correct mistakes, thinking it can be bad for morale. But having to replace employees is much harder on morale than taking the time to make corrections. Remember, corrections shouldn't be given in anger, and if you wait to correct behavior until you are angry, it will be difficult to strip your feelings from your comments. But mistakes that are corrected by a leader—a teacher—who is fair, knowledgeable, and patient quickly disappear. There is also something inherently simple, noble, and modest about a leader who sees his role as teacher, not as boss. The teacher's function is to help the student to be their best; a boss views his employees as helping the boss achieve his own goals. Coach Wooden wanted his players to know that they were working *with* him, not for him.

Perhaps the best decision I made while working at CBS was to spend a great deal of time with my two top creative executives, teaching them how I expected them to do their jobs. In the television business, a tremendous amount of money, energy, and focus is spent trying to sell a television pilot—but in most instances, the minute a pilot is ordered to series, the top executives hand off responsibility to the lowest-ranking member of their team. I made it a point to work in tandem with them, supervising each episode for the entire first year a series was on the air. It was an ideal teaching environment, and a process that we all found enjoyable. When I moved off the show in the second year, my executives had really learned how to manage the creative oversight of the series through demonstration, imitation, correction, and repetition.

SECRET #8

GAME TIME IS WHEN THE COACH'S JOB
IS ALMOST OVER

THIS SECRET sounds almost blasphemous in our age of micromanaging coaches, color commentators, and so called experts, but the fact is, Coach Wooden did very little coaching once the game started. There was simply no question that the players knew exactly what was expected of them, and how they needed to perform. The players were never told to just "keep it close," and their coach would think of something at the end. Though there can be no doubt that Coach Wooden is the greatest coach of all time, he was never better than a decent "game coach." In fact, Coach told me that he hoped that "once the game starts, I could go up in the stands and the team wouldn't miss me." To some, this sounds preposterous. I would suggest that this is one of his greatest secrets.

Coach Wooden's locker room speeches before games were pretty straightforward: a brief overview of the team we were playing, a remarkably short description of the key players on the opponent's team, and an exhortation to make sure we put out a maximum effort. As Bill Walton recalls, he would then say, "I've done my job. The rest is up to you. Don't be looking over here at the sideline." The result was the empowerment of the people who now had to go out and perform. It was actually an interestingly choreographed transition of power from practice, where Coach was in total control, to the game, where the players had to take charge. It was also an unspoken yet powerful way to communicate his trust in his players to execute what he had taught them. And it worked to perfection.

Unlike most of the coaches you see today, John Wooden actually sat in his seat during games instead of standing up and prowling the sidelines. It was extremely rare for him ever to yell at his players during a game, and he always projected a sense of composure from the bench. He did not want his players looking over at the bench for a signal or directions; he wanted them to be in charge. That confidence was there because the teaching was done in practice, and game time was an opportunity to put those lessons into action. With no fear about outcome, but with a clear sense that effort was the true goal, that confidence was a cornerstone of the Bruins' remarkable success.

Bill Walton describes this unique quality of Coach Wooden's by saying, "People always had this sense that Coach was conservative, a strict disciplinarian, a total control freak. But in truth he was about individual freedom, creativity, and imagination. He was about giving the responsibility to everyone else, to let them perform. What made it work so beautifully was that we all became extensions of his mind, his vision, and his dreams." Everything that Coach expected of his players had been internalized by them, and he was secure enough in that to let them command the stage.

How many businesses can barely function when the boss isn't there? And when he is there, every decision has to be approved, every detail reviewed, and every final draft redone to the head honcho's liking. Without a doubt, in an extremely small business, this may be practical. But even in the case of a small company, this type of management is bad for morale and stifles initiative and creativity. People need to learn how to think for themselves, not merely guess what the boss would do. Coach understood that once the game started, his job was nearly over. But most managers are simply too insecure to adopt this system; they feel they need to have more control when the heat is on. Yet UCLA basketball teams were the most controlled and balanced teams I've ever seen, and the key was that Coach gained control by relinquishing it. Pretty "Zen-like" for an old Midwestern guy like Coach, but in hindsight he could teach Phil Jackson a thing or two about being a Zen Master!

Particularly when your job involves overseeing a creative process, it's essential that your creative team sense your confidence in them through your willingness to step aside and let their vision take shape. I think this principle is one of the greatest gifts that Coach Wooden passed along to me. Understanding that creative people are often extremely insecure, I made it a habit to be inconspicuous and deferential on the sets of the programs I worked on. Though by title I was the "boss," in truth my important decisions had already been made: The scripts were done, the professionals hired, the actors in their places. Though it might have helped stoke my own ego to bark out instructions and act important, once filming began it was time for my "players" to shine. What they needed from me at that point was not more input, but a sense of confidence and assurance that the show was going to be terrific. Creative people know when you trust them. So if you want them to be creative, *trust them.*

SECRET #9

A GREAT LEADER CANNOT WORRY
ABOUT BEING WELL LIKED

DURING MY YEARS of playing for Coach, I can honestly say that many of his players didn't like him, though I never felt that he disliked us back. No doubt, he liked some more than others, but he wasn't one to socialize and schmooze. In fact, Coach later told me, "I don't think all of them ever liked me. But they're not going to like you when you make decisions that affect them." In many ways, I think that Coach also understood all too well that his job depended on the team's performance, not on how much the guys on the team liked him. He needed to be a firm disciplinarian, which is hardly the way to ingratiate yourself with a bunch of guys in college. He corrected, cajoled, and even yelled at times. I suspect that Coach suffered internally with the knowledge that kids were being hurt and lives were being altered, but he never changed his ways or his demeanor. Of course, the ultimate irony of this secret is that many years after graduating, there are countless players who never really liked Coach when they were playing for him but who now will tell you they love him.

Coach could be very tough on players, particularly those he felt needed to be pushed. Compared to guys like Bobby Knight and Pat Riley, Coach was pretty mild-mannered, but he could needle pretty relentlessly to try to get a player to change his ways. In my junior year in school, Coach was on our starting center, Steve Patterson, in almost every practice. Steve had the bad habit of waving the ball around a bit when he caught it, and this often led to turnovers. Coach would explode at Steve, sometimes blaming Steve for spending too much time at night "catting around" (which we figured must have been some sort of Indiana-speak). We even started calling Steve "The Cat Man" and "El Gato" in honor of Coach's continual references to his nighttime activities.

Finally, Steve felt he couldn't take it anymore. Without informing anyone on the team, Steve made plans to leave school. Purely by chance, my best friend, John Ecker, and I bumped into Steve in the parking lot near Pauley Pavilion just as he was leaving for the airport. He had booked a flight out of town. John and I spent the next few hours convincing Steve to stay in school. We understood why Steve was angry at Coach; we didn't feel too good toward Coach either. But John and I knew that Steve was a key to the team's success, and he was making a big mistake personally. What was truly amazing about this is that John Ecker was our top reserve; if Steve left school, John would have immediately become a starter. But John was committed to the team, and so we talked Steve into staying in school. The capper on this is that Steve ended up scoring 29 points in the NCAA championship game against Villanova. We never could have won it without him.

On a certain level, it was only inevitable that Coach

had some players who were not fond of him, and he actually expected it. Since Coach only played seven players extensively, that meant he always had at least five guys who were displeased—and he wouldn't want it any other way. You see, the guys at UCLA who weren't playing were often players who had been recruited by dozens of other schools, and could have played almost anywhere except at UCLA. In fact, many years after we had graduated, Bill Walton introduced me to his wife, Lori, by saying that when we played together our second string was the second best team in the country! The bench players were just as competitive as the players on the floor, and the amount of ability separating them from being a star was often too small for a young person to comprehend. But Coach Wooden counted on these players' burning desire to get them to come to practice and give a tremendous effort

It was no surprise to Coach that in many instances the bench players didn't like him. Despite what has often been written about Coach, he actually was not a star every year he played, so he could relate to the unhappiness of his reserves. When young John was a sophomore in high school, his coach didn't let him start. He got so upset at one point in the season that he removed his shoes and clothing in the gymnasium and walked off the floor, threatening to transfer. He was furious over being relegated to the role of sixth man. But despite his threat, he didn't quit, and he didn't transfer. That burning desire helped him become the best high school player in Indiana his junior and senior years in high school. But those who think John Wooden doesn't know the pain of not playing are wrong; he knew from firsthand experience how upset these players were going to be, just like he knew that every team needs backups who are burning with the desire to play. The hard part is accepting this pain as a natural and unavoidable part of managing a team with depth and talent.

Before moving on from this point, it is essential that you understand what this means for your organization. Hoping that everyone is happy all the time is not a realistic outlook. It will never happen, no matter what you do. A strong leader understands that this is something he has to accept. John Wooden is not a mean guy, but he had to keep his emotional distance from some youngsters who would have really liked some nurturing and stroking. He has told me many times that he not only understands why I was unhappy not playing, he expected me to be unhappy, and wouldn't want me on his team if I wasn't unhappy. As a youngster, I thought that was sort of cruel; as an adult, I understand his point, and I realize that being an effective leader is not as easy as it looks. One of Coach Wooden's heroes, Abraham Lincoln, put it well when he said, "Most anyone can stand adversity. But to test a person's character, give them power."

The idea of being disliked is tough to accept if you are a real "people pleaser," since making others happy is of paramount importance to you. This will be especially true if your ability to please people has played a role in your rise to a position of power. But being a leader means making tough choices about whose happiness matters and whose doesn't. Feelings get hurt and lives are disrupted, but the ability to make those tough choices is essential to being an effective leader. This is not to be confused with the behavior of some coaches who yell and scream demeaning comments in an attempt to toughen up their troops; Coach argues that those people are more dictators than leaders, and there is a big difference.

Another aspect of the leader's difficult role is that there can be only one clear leader of the group, and that person must be willing to accept responsibility for the actions of all. While it is the leader's job to divert praise to others in the organization, it is also his job to accept responsibility for the failures of the group. This might place you in conflict with people you do business with, but it's important that you be willing to be the lightning rod for those who may be displeased with something your team has done. Early in my television career, a woman working for me made a statement in a sales meeting at a network that infuriated the head of the largest talent agency in Hollywood. This agent was incredibly powerful, and no one in their right mind would want him mad at them. But when I was told about the situation, I immediately called this man up and accepted complete responsibility for the mistake. Mad as he was, it just wasn't much fun for him to be mad at me, since I hadn't even been in the meeting. In fact, I think that after accepting my apology, he actually had a much higher opinion of me, since I had made it clear I was willing for him to be angry with me. Being the leader requires you to shoulder the blame, and that can be a highly unpleasant task. But there is a positive side to this behavior, because a leader who takes the heat for the mistakes of his underlings invariably develops great loyalty in those who are expected to follow him.

One other pitfall you must avoid is to become too enmeshed in the personal lives of your underlings. You should recognize the individuality of your people and treat them accordingly, but your values and expectations are the ones that matter, and they should be clear to everyone in your organization. Bill Walton and I were struck by how we had the exact same impression of Coach Wooden despite our remarkably dissimilar experiences. Bill was a three-time College Player of the Year, while I was a little-used reserve; Bill played center and is seven feet tall (but he always claimed to be "only" 6'11"), while I played guard at six feet (though I always stretched the truth and claimed to be 6'1")—and yet, from these opposite perspectives, when we looked at our coach we saw the same man. When I told this to Coach, he was clearly pleased. Coach has been complimented and flattered for so long that he rarely lets on that such comments are meaningful to him, but the fact that Bill and I viewed him so similarly reflected something important about his ways. Coach never got very close to any of us, whether we were benchwarmers or All-Americans. Though it was only human that he liked some players more than others, it was pretty hard for any of us to have a sense of whether or not he actually liked you. Of course, Coach had a great saying to explain his approach, one he borrowed from the famous football coach Amos Alonzo Stagg: He simply said, "I like some more than others, but I love them all the same."

SECRET #10

GREAT LEADERS GIVE CREDIT TO OTHERS, BUT ACCEPT THE BLAME THEMSELVES

COACH REALIZED that players, not coaches, win games, and he always deflected the press's attention away from himself and onto us. He was acutely aware of how sensitive the egos and psyches of his kids were, and he knew that they were the ones who needed to shoot, defend, and rebound. When postgame interviewers clamored for Coach to describe the turning point in a game, he never claimed that a change of defense or a great substitution turned the tide. Coach instinctively knew that by giving credit where it was due, his players would be happier and would win more games.

Of all the secrets revealed in this book, this one is perhaps the only one that Coach struggled with from time to time. There were certainly occasions when Coach didn't give sufficient credit to some of his outstanding assistant coaches. Many people know that Jerry Norman, a man responsible for much of the success of the UCLA program, never felt he got the credit he deserved. Many of Coach's reserve players, myself included, could have used a public pat on the back once in a while. Still, I honestly think John

Wooden sincerely believes he did credit his assistants and substitutes more than he actually did. He certainly believes that a good leader does redirect credit. Coach is the first to admit he isn't perfect, and perhaps he should have done a better job of putting these valuable contributors in the spotlight; this is one of the few areas where his actions may have fallen short of his principles.

Coach did clearly understand the need to go out of his way to praise the players who did the little things that make teams win. Getting players to shoot the ball was easy; he knew that the media would invariably focus on the leading scorer or the guy who scored the winning basket, so Coach would go out of his way to single out a player who had made a key steal, grabbed a big rebound, or played strong and consistent defense. Giving credit publicly is the most visible form of positive reinforcement available to any leader; by using it strategically and judiciously, you can encourage the behavior you're trying to bring out in your whole team. Not everyone can be a star, and you don't want people thinking they have to be in order to earn your praise. Go the extra mile to single out the unnoticed contributions, and you'll inspire everyone to give their best efforts, knowing they'll be appreciated; the more widely recognized accomplishments are generally self-reinforcing and don't need as much encouragement from the leader.

An important corollary to this is that the effective leader must always be willing to shoulder the blame for the shortcomings of his team. After all, every decision must ultimately be approved by the boss, so the boss must not look to deflect blame on those who made suggestions. Of course, that's why it is so much tougher to be the person in charge who has to decide, as opposed to an assistant whose role is to suggest. Everyone on the team has been selected and approved by the head coach, so it doesn't make sense to blame the players that you chose. It takes a strong leader to accept the blame, but your organization will appreciate the strength it takes, and will reward it with loyalty. Perhaps the toughest loss in UCLA history was in Bill Walton's senior year, when the talented and favored Bruins lost to David Thompson's North Carolina State team in the NCAA semifinals. There must be hundreds of reasons why UCLA lost that game. But Coach Wooden accepts full responsibility for that game, saying that his failure to call a timeout and make adjustments was the reason for the loss. It still rankles him some twenty-five years later.

Crediting others is of paramount importance when you're involved in any creative endeavor. The people in your organization must feel your approval and support to do their best work. So if your goal is for your unit to function at its best, and you're confident that as the group leader you'll get the rewards you're due when the group achieves its goals, then follow this secret. The leader who focuses attention on his own exploits and accomplishments is often better known than some of his more accomplished peers, but he'll rarely get the rest of his organization to perform at its peak. I always went out of my way to thank the director of photography for a great shot he had made, or the casting director for an exciting discovery she had found, or a production designer for a particularly inventive set. These people are all well-paid professionals, but it always amazed me how much they appreciated the personal touch of being praised for a job well done. I know that after these encounters, these people always went the extra mile to make their part of the production really shine.

In show business, it's almost normal for executives to try to take the credit for every program they're even marginally connected to. I tried to always make a point of correcting people when they would congratulate me for "creating" or "producing" programs like *Touched by an Angel, Caroline in the City, Rescue 911,* and *Dr. Quinn, Medicine Woman.* Most people in my position not only don't correct people who use these terms to describe their role, they use those terms themselves. I supervised the development and production of those shows, and I was ultimately responsible for hiring everyone who worked on the programs—but it was the talented writers and producers who had the right to feel that *they* were the creators and producers. While this may seem a small distinction to the majority of people who aren't used to the terminology, I felt that it would be rude to try to take credit from those who deserve it. Maybe my reputation suffered because I was unwilling to grab all the credit I could. But as Coach would say, "Be more concerned with your character than your reputation. Character is what you really are; reputation is what you are perceived to be."

SECRET #11

SEEK CONSISTENCY—AVOID PEAKS
AND VALLEYS

THIS IS ANOTHER trait that made Coach unique, but few people outside the UCLA program understood how totally he adhered to this philosophy. Most coaches aim for emotional peaks by giving inspirational speeches. From Pat O'Brien's famous "Win one for the Gipper" speech in the Ronald Reagan classic *Knute Rockne, All American* to Gene Hackman's rousing halftime speech in that great basketball film *Hoosiers,* the role of the coach was to fire up the troops. Coach Wooden, on the other hand, never resorted to emotionalism. He was, in fact, oddly businesslike (a strange term, since so few people in the business world are actually "businesslike"). He wanted a consistent effort, and knew that there was always a valley beyond every peak. He expected tremendous effort on a regular basis.

"Getting up for a game" is commonplace in sports. Stories abound of players throwing up in locker rooms, banging their heads into walls, and generally acting like rabid dogs. Since effort in the UCLA program was expected at all times, the key to preparing for games was to be focused. This is substantially different than being "up" for a game, which suggests a high degree of emotionality. Focus implies calm, intelligent, laserlike attention, and those who marveled at the precision action of the well-oiled UCLA basketball teams could tell that focus, and not emotion, was our driving force. Coach was not manic; he was always calm and measured. He set the tone and we followed. (My high school coach, Courtney Borio, who played for Wooden in the early 1950s, took this one step further: When a game was tense, the crowd was roaring, and the gym was rocking, Coach Borio would always *lower* his voice during timeouts. He seemed so calm it actually settled us down.) Staying on an even keel helped us execute with precision when other teams let the excitement of the moment lead to bad shots and turnovers.

Never was this goal of consistency clearer than when you watched a Wooden-coached team win a big game. Just before the end of the game, Coach would always remind us not to make fools of ourselves in the postgame hysteria. There was never any excessive celebration by the players; we left that up to the fans. In fact, I think Coach Wooden is every bit as proud of the way his players conducted themselves *after* winning the championships as he is of the fact that they won the championship at all. This philosophy of avoiding peaks and valleys is also an outgrowth of Coach's extremely long-range view of life: He was acutely aware that the journey was going to continue for both his players and his coaching staff. Winning a championship was a worthy accomplishment, but it did not signal an end of something, but rather a part of a much longer continuum. When interviewers asked

Coach if he was thrilled, ecstatic, or overjoyed, they were always disappointed to hear Coach say that he was simply "pleased." He left the emotional hyperbole to others.

Organizations can learn from this principle, since most managers do not accept that valleys follow peaks. They expect one peak to follow another, and this leads to burnout and poor morale. Peaks and valleys are an intrinsic part of the human condition. It's up to the group leader to stay calm, emphasize focus and continuous effort, and never lose sight of long-term goals. The manager who accepts the reality of emotional cycles and creates a framework within it will do much better in the long run than the hard-driving emotional autocrat who expects his workers to maintain and even build on their fever pitch. It is also important to integrate another one of Coach's favorite expressions when trying to even out your peaks and valleys, and that is his saying, "If we magnified blessings as much as we magnify disappointments, we would all be much happier." It's all too easy to allow yourself to brood about bad news; it is equally important to feel good about triumphs. The key is to keep all moods from swinging to extremes—good advice for life as well as business.

I had subconsciously integrated this message from Coach early in my career, and I'm glad I did. The first television movie I had a credit on was in the early 1980s. It was a distinctly unmemorable movie as I look back nearly two decades later, and it wasn't particularly thrilling at the time, either. What I do recall clearly was my role in it, and what I learned from it. The movie was called *Incident at Crestridge,* and it was originally supposed to be based on a true story. We had acquired the rights to the story of a woman who was elected sheriff in a corrupt small town in Nevada. What we hadn't counted on was that the bad guys in the story had never been convicted of the crimes they were accused of committing in our screenplay. No insurance company was going to write a policy for the film, and so we had to fictionalize the story before filming. Since the television writers were on strike at the time, the job of rewriting fell to yours truly. In very little time, I had sufficiently rewritten the script so we could go forward. In addition to fictionalizing all of the characters, I had to modify much of the dialogue. But as the man responsible for the new script, I was painfully aware of its shortcomings. Imagine my surprise when a review for the film singled out my sharp and natural dialogue as the strongest point of what the reviewer thought was a terrific movie. Friends who read the review in the trades called me up with great excitement and enthusiasm, and they were surprised that I wasn't nearly as ecstatic as they expected. But I knew the reviewer was wrong, and I saved that clipping for many years. When the reviews for *Dr. Quinn* (a show I loved and thought was going to work) were generally bad, I retrieved that clipping and reminded myself that you shouldn't get too carried away when the news is good—or bad. Avoid those peaks and valleys, and have confidence in your own judgment.

SECRET #12

FAIRNESS IS GIVING ALL PEOPLE THE TREATMENT *THEY EARN AND DESERVE*

PERHAPS NONE of the secrets contained in this book is potentially more troublesome than this one. In fact, it's fair to say that this principle was the cause of so many players' unhappiness at UCLA, mine included, because we didn't understand that a basketball team is not intended to be a place of absolute social equality. There were times when reserves on the team were punished for infractions as minor as throwing water balloons in hotel rooms, or for being minutes late for meals, while our counterparts on the team who were All-Americans occasionally had infractions like these (and worse) overlooked. How could such "unfair" enforcement fit in with the sense that John Wooden was the fairest man in America?

Many of us remained perplexed and even bitter about this disparity until many years after we graduated, when we were forced to run a company or lead a group. Faced with that type of responsibility, we saw that Coach Wooden's methods made perfect sense. While Coach is often praised for being a highly moral, almost saintly leader, it is important to understand that he had a practical side as well. He may have viewed himself primarily as a teacher, but he knew that he was being paid to win basketball games, the fans expected him to win basketball games, and in order to do that he needed to keep his best players on the court if at all possible. Weighing the pros and cons in this type of situation is among the toughest calculations a leader has to make.

Clearly, Coach understood that certain players were so vital to the success of the team that he had to balance enforcing rules with the effect of doing so on the outcome of the game. When you sit out a Kareem Abdul-Jabbar or a Bill Walton, you don't just punish them, you punish the entire team in their desire to win. Larry Farmer, a former teammate of mine who has gone on to a successful college coaching career, tells a great story about this dilemma that exemplifies Coach Wooden's delicate approach to such decisions. At the time, Larry was a very young head coach at UCLA (barely thirty) and was working in the long shadow that the Wooden legend left behind. The trainer at UCLA was the legendary Elvin "Ducky" Drake, who had been there from the time John Wooden arrived in Westwood. It was Ducky's job to do bed checks, and he took the job seriously. The night before the final game of Farmer's first season as head coach, the team's leading scorer was not in his bed when Ducky came by to check on him. By this time, Ducky was in his eighties and had heard some pretty tall tales from ballplayers, so rather than leave and be subject to some predictable excuse from the player (I was on the balcony; I was under the bed; I was in the shower), Ducky simply got in the player's bed and went to sleep. At 3:00 A.M., the player returned and woke Ducky up. There was not a single excuse that could make this go away.

The next morning, Ducky broke the bad news to young Coach Farmer. Farmer was well aware that Ducky was also testing his mettle to see if he would stand up to the player. No doubt Larry thought hard about Coach Wooden's leadership, and then stood tall and did what he thought Coach Wooden would do: This youngster may have been the leading scorer, but he had broken a rule, and so Larry sat him out for the entire final game. The game was close and the Bruins played hard, but they eventually went down to defeat. Shortly thereafter, Farmer visited Coach, and the subject of the disciplinary action came up. Larry expected Coach to praise him for his backbone and commitment to enforcing the rules, so he was surprised when Coach told him he would have handled it differently. Confused, Larry asked Coach, "What would you have done?" Coach responded that he absolutely would have sat the player out—*but only for the first half.* It's one thing to have rules and enforce them, but you have to balance that with the expectations that are placed on you to win. Of course, if the player in question was a bench player, a full-game suspension would have been applied without a moment's hesitation. Pragmatism and principles can make for tough decisions, but leaders have to take them on and keep moving.

When I was at CBS, I sometimes had to give certain people a level of consideration that I simply would not have given anyone else. One instance involved Chuck Norris, the popular star of *Walker, Texas Ranger.* As the title of the show suggests, the program was shot on location in Dallas, Texas. At least a couple of times a year, I would hop on a plane to spend a few hours face-to-face with Chuck. He's an honest and straightforward guy, but he had been a major feature film star, and was understandably used to special handling. I found that long-distance phone calls just did not work if I wanted the kind of personal trust and commitment I needed to have with Chuck. One time, during a small crisis with the production, I flew down to Dallas to see Chuck so we could sort out the problem. On my way out to the set, I got a phone call from my boss at the network, who couldn't understand why I had to fly all the way to Dallas to work out a solution. He didn't see the need to give special consideration to certain crucial people. Needless to say, Chuck always appreciated the personal attention I gave him and was a complete pleasure to work with. Right from the start, our direct lines of communication helped us solve a much bigger problem than this one, something I'll go into later.

In a different but similar situation, we hired a relatively unknown actress by the name of Roma Downey to star in *Touched by an Angel*. Critics and pundits unanimously agreed that this series would fail, but somehow, perhaps miraculously, the series got picked up for a second season. I had come to know Roma as an intelligent, thoughtful, and forceful individual in our dealings, and as we were starting our second season she called me directly with a concern over her contract. Normally, I would have simply told an actress that her deal was her deal, and she would have to live with it. It was vital that my business people know that I would support them when we had a signed deal, and 99 percent of the time I did. But Roma had proven to me that she was not just some hysterical performer, and despite the fact that my own business affairs executives begged me to stay out of the matter, I flew up to Salt Lake City to meet with her. As she outlined her concerns, I found her arguments compelling, logical, and fair. When I returned to Los Angeles, I insisted to my business affairs people that we adjust her deal to reflect the concerns she had shared with me. We did have a signed contract, and by all rights we could have insisted that she adhere to it. But she had demonstrated to me that she deserved to be taken seriously, and had made her case with great skill. Did I give her the same treatment that I would have given most other actors in the same situation? Absolutely not! As I've said, in most cases I would have told them they had a signed deal, and they had to live with it. But I also knew that as the show became a bigger hit, Roma would become a bigger star. I was right on both counts. Fortunately, Coach had taught me that you don't treat everyone the same. I didn't enjoy learning that lesson, but I certainly did benefit from it.

SECRET #13

THE TEAM THAT MAKES THE MOST MISTAKES . . . WINS!

Now I promised to give you some of the Wizard's secrets, but my guess is that when you read this one you started to wonder if this is all a joke. Actually, this is far from a joke, though it does require a bit of an explanation. Many years ago, Coach played for a man named Piggy Lambert at Purdue University, and this phrase actually came from Coach Lambert. Naturally, no coach is looking to encourage mistakes, but this saying applies to the only type of mistake that is acceptable: mistakes of *commission*. If you were doing something positive, and it resulted in a turnover, you were rarely criticized. If the mistake was on something we had gone over many times before—like failing to pull up at the free throw line on a fast break, or throwing a crosscourt pass—that was *not* acceptable. But basketball, like business, presents people with countless new situations to assess and act upon quickly. Aggressive and confident people are bound to make some errors in these situations. As Coach would say, "The man who is afraid to risk failure seldom has to face success."

Coach summarized this idea pretty concisely when he told me, "You're going to make mistakes. We are all imperfect. We are going to make mistakes. But learning from them, that's what's important. Hopefully you won't repeat the same mistake over and over. My Dad tried to get across to me in grade school that I should never try to be better than someone else. Now if you just stop there, it is kind of crazy advice. But he didn't stop there. He said to learn from others and never cease trying to be the best that you can be. That is under your control; the other isn't. So don't worry about being *better,* worry about being the best *you* can be. Part of being your best is accepting your own mistakes and learning from them. But do not be afraid to fail."

What Coach was most concerned with when he repeated this saying is that no one should try to play mistake-free basketball. Basketball is a game of quickness and reactions, and mistakes are inevitable. But many coaches inculcate such a fear of mistakes in their players that they play like automatons. To play freely and quickly, you have to embrace initiative and risk-taking, so long as they're within the prescribed general framework. But there was one type of mistake that was *guaranteed* to get Coach yelling, "Goodness gracious, sakes alive" at you: that was when you made a mistake and then committed another mistake because you were still angry about the first one. How often do you see a player make a bad pass and then commit a silly foul trying to steal the ball because they're upset? If your players know they are free to make mistakes, they also have to be mature enough to let them go as soon as they're made. The team that makes the most mistakes may not always win, but a team that tries to make no mistakes hardly ever will.

Coach also readily admits that he made many mistakes with every team he ever taught. This was true whether the team went undefeated or had just a decent season. He put it humorously when he told me, "I hope my last year of teaching I was better than the year before. I'd like to think I got better at teaching every year. So when I started out, I must have been *really* lousy." Now, John Wooden was never a lousy coach, but he did make mistakes, accepted that he would continue to make them, and understood that his players were going to make mistakes, too. This attitude created a sense of freedom for Bruin players. It is ludicrous to expect quickness and no mistakes, and Coach always wanted quickness.

Basketball, like many businesses, is ultimately a creative enterprise, and creativity cannot flourish in a sterile, autocratic environment. Too many people in business situations are not engaged in trying to do their task the best way they possibly can; they're simply trying to execute what they presume the boss's vision is for them. These people become tentative, more concerned with trying to intuit someone else's idea than with quickly doing it the way they think it should be done. This doesn't mean that if someone in your organization continually does things wrong you should tolerate their mistakes. No, you should fire that person immediately. But if you have a good group of people working under you, and have set up a system of checks and balances so that people can only make mistakes commensurate with their job level in the company, then you have to accept that they will make mistakes. If the thinking that led to the wrong decision makes sense, then you should correct that mistake, but in a positive and enthusiastic tone. If someone makes mistakes while trying to win, that can be tolerated—but there should be no tolerance for mistakes that are made to keep from losing. It is your job, as the manager, to know the difference and to make sure your employees do, too.

This brings to mind something that happened while we were doing the second year of *Dr. Quinn*. The program had been an overnight success in spite of the critics' early resistance, and we started the second year with even higher expectations. Perhaps the most expensive and important choices you make when producing a television series are the writers you choose each year. They make the show great . . . or awful. Our executive producer had pushed hard for us to let her hire a high-priced writer she felt would be perfect for the show. We went along with her recommendation, made a costly deal, and then less than four weeks later the executive producer called back to say she had made a big mistake and we needed to replace this star writer. My two top development executives, Kelly Goode and Glenn Adilman, were in my office in a flash trying to get my help in talking some sense into this executive producer. They were both surprised when I told them that we had made a mistake, that we should accept it and move on. In fact, they were sort of stunned when I actually applauded the courage of our mistaken executive producer. But Coach had taught me that mistakes are part of the game, and if they're mistakes of commission you must accept them.

In the twenty-first century, the speed at which information flows and the business landscape changes demand a degree of daring that would have been inconceivable just a few decades ago. The term "businesslike" described a sense of caution, conservatism, even stodginess. Today, these words are applied to those businesses that have lagged behind the rest in a world of change. Nowhere is this atmosphere of risk-taking more evident than in Silicon Valley, where failure and risk are embraced as an integral part of developing the next big idea or revolutionary concept. This type of culture can only flourish if management clearly communicates its acceptance of failure. Ideas that are new are by definition untested, untried, and risky. Much of our culture, and the vast majority of our educational process, is focused on elimination of mistakes and dissent. Any business that wants to counteract these institutionalized and internalized thought patterns needs to do so *actively*. Most great ideas, when first considered, seem crazy to some people involved in evaluating them. But you cannot be frightened by the prospect of being wildly wrong, or you'll run the risk of never being wildly right.

SECRET #14

SURROUND YOURSELF WITH STRONG, OPINIONATED PEOPLE

C OACH WOODEN always had the best assistant coaches in the business. Many people who played for the early championship teams will tell you that Jerry Norman is probably the best man never to be a head coach in major college basketball. While I was in school, Denny Crum (the longtime great head coach at the University of Louisville) and Dr. Gary Cunningham (the athletic director at the University of California at Santa Barbara whose two-year coaching record at UCLA was an astounding 56-8), two incredibly talented men, were the top assistants. Coach Crum and Coach Wooden often saw things differently, and anyone who knows Denny would know that he was strong-willed and persistent. As Coach told me, "You don't want yes-men around you, all they do is inflate your ego. Most leaders already have a pretty big ego, so having people around who inflate it more does you no good at all." But Coach would be the first to tell you that while he wanted to be challenged on his decisions, his assistants clearly understood that ultimately every decision was up to the head coach.

Coach also made sure his players gave the assistant coaches the respect he felt they were due. He made it a point to occasionally leave practice and put one of his assistants in charge (though many times he just snuck up to the top of the arena and watched from there). This sent a clear message to the players that he truly trusted these men. It is also interesting to note that his belief in having strong-willed people working for him extended to the trainers, and even the players. I was at a reunion not too long ago that included players from about a ten-year period from the late 1960s through the 1970s, an incredibly diverse group of people who had gone on to work in many fields. I was struck by the fact that we all seemed so comfortable with each other after many years had passed. I mentioned this to Andre McCarter, who had been a star guard in the mid-1970s, and he attributed it to the fact that we were all a really honest, outspoken group of guys. No hidden agendas, no gossip behind people's backs, just direct, blunt, and clear points of view. I think Andre understood this secret of the Pyramid before I did.

To some degree, the way Coach Wooden recruited players added to the strong-willed nature of his teams. Unlike most coaches who employ flattery and ego stroking, Coach Wooden left some recruits unsure that he even wanted them to come to UCLA. Ken Heitz, who became a starting guard on three national championship teams in the 1960s, tells a story of his recruitment that underscores this point. Heitz was an All-American at Righetti High School, in Santa Maria, California, where he averaged 28 points and 15 rebounds a game. In general, recruiting trips were a giant ego boost for young Ken. But when John Wooden "recruited" him, he told Ken that he had all the tools to be an ideal sixth man. Rather than tell Ken that he would start, shoot a lot, and make a great pro like every other coach Ken spoke with, John Wooden told him he probably wouldn't even be a starter. For many young men, that would have been the perfect excuse to go to some school where they really wanted him. But Ken was challenged by Coach's forecast, and he came to Westwood intent on proving him wrong. While this approach might not work with every youngster, it did the trick with players who had confidence in their abilities and a strong ego to go with it. It was almost as if Coach Wooden's undersell was a part of a natural selection process in which the weak and timid were weeded out before they even got to Westwood.

The fact that players as well as assistant coaches had strong personalities was sometimes a deciding factor in games, since players felt empowered to make suggestions about strategy. Perhaps the most dramatic example of this was the NCAA Finals that matched UCLA against the Jacksonville team that featured 7' forward Pembroke Burrows III and 7'2" center Artis Gilmore. Entering the game, Coach Wooden's strategy was to put a player in front of Gilmore and try to make them throw over that man into the post. In the first ten minutes of the game, this wasn't working at all. Sidney Wicks, always outspoken, suggested to Coach that even though he wasn't much more than 6'8", he should be allowed to guard the much taller Gilmore from behind. Though it seemed like a crazy idea, Coach Wooden went along with Sidney's suggestion. As it happened, the whole game turned around from that moment on. The officials, perhaps as surprised by the move as Artis Gilmore was, allowed Sidney to get away with multiple blocks that should have been ruled goaltending, and the Bruins quickly regained the lead. When the game was over and we had won, Coach Wooden was praised for his ingenious strategy. Coach was happy to let reporters know that this ingenious strategy was not his idea, but a suggestion from Sidney Wicks. In truth, it was his strategy, since he was ultimately responsible for saying yes or no. Knowing when to listen is the key, but it was because his personnel felt free to make suggestions that Coach won his fourth straight national title.

Coach not only believed in following the NCAA recruiting rules, he imposed even more stringent rules on his assistants. Fortunately, as strong personalities, they were capable of defying Coach's directives when necessary. Winning basketball games requires talented players (remember Secret Number 1), and recruiting them was mainly the job of the assistant coaches. Coach Wooden did not like to recruit, and it required some real ingenuity on the part of his assistants to keep bringing in the top high school players in the country. As I've mentioned, one of Coach Wooden's personal rules was that he would not recruit any out-of-state players who didn't contact him first. Now, many players who came to UCLA from out of state did write and express interest, but Gary Cunningham and Denny Crum weren't about to pass on potential recruits just because they hadn't written UCLA a letter. So they devised a system of sending a letter supposedly written by the potential recruit to a contact who lived in the same state as the youngster. That contact would then put that letter in an envelope and send it to John Wooden.

Coach Wooden would go see Denny or Gary and ask them if the kid was worth recruiting. The toughest part of the whole process was keeping a straight face as they promised to "look into it" to see how good the young player was! They were independent and strong-willed enough to defy Coach when they were sure it was in his best interest.

Far too many managers, insecure in their place on the organizational ladder, only hire people they can intimidate and subjugate. They may give lip service to encouraging people to speak up, but they know that their underlings are so timid that they would never challenge their boss's authority. But a leader who is secure that he alone will ultimately decide what direction to take is never threatened when someone questions his decisions. In fact, a good leader is always open to revising the plan if someone can poke a hole in it or suggest a better alternative. If the boss's door is closed to criticism, you can be sure that criticism will turn up in whispers at the water cooler and behind closed doors. But there's a fine line that must be maintained; employees must understand that they're totally free to challenge and question any decision, but they cannot be allowed to question your authority.

When Ken Heitz played for Coach Wooden, he got a strong lesson in what happens when an employee or player crosses over the fine line to questioning authority. After Heitz made a suggestion in private about the type of offense the Bruins should use to attack the Oregon State zone, Wooden seized on it and made the change. Not only did the suggestion work, but Coach gave Heitz credit for the change in the next day's papers. Emboldened by this development, Heitz yelled over to Coach during the next game suggesting another strategic change. Unlike his suggestion the week before, this one resulted in Wooden yelling back at Heitz to leave the coaching to him. As a youngster, Heitz was confused by the seeming inconsistency of Coach Wooden's two reactions; years later, when Heitz was responsible for managing a large law firm, the difference was clear: In the first case, the suggestion was made in private, while in the second case, it was made in front of the team, the crowd, and the press table. While it's important for a leader to be open to suggestions, it is equally important that those questioning the leader never appear to question the leader's authority. What made little sense to young Ken Heitz, the player, made perfect sense to Ken when he was an adult in the business world.

It is an absolute given that people in your organization would do things differently if they were in charge. Recommending something is always easier than having to actually decide what to do. If you hire smart people, they'll often give you a great idea that is worth implementing immediately. If they believe in you as a leader, they'll also understand when you listen to their ideas and reject them. But there are always people who are dangerous cancers who ultimately not only question your direction, but wonder whether you should be the one making the decisions at all. This is a real organizational dilemma, but if you have someone on your team who has a problem with the fact that you're the boss and he isn't, it's imperative that you send him on his way. Naturally, if this person is talented, you should do everything in your power to get him to lend you his support, but when it reaches the point where you know that isn't going to happen, you're out of options. So long as you keep this distinction in mind, having strong people who express their opinions and aren't merely looking to reflect yours is one of the keys to the success of any team.

SECRET #15

TEAMWORK IS NOT A PREFERENCE, IT'S A NECESSITY

I REMEMBER being struck by how UCLA players always acknowledged a teammate when a pass led to a basket. It seemed so selfless and natural. This trait was taught, and was absolutely expected by Coach. If you weren't interested in playing team ball, UCLA was just not going to be the school for you. In fact, when John Wooden evaluated high school players as potential recruits, team attitude was one of the most important traits he tried to assess through both observation and recommendations. Wooden knew that if he could get quick players working as a unit, their group quickness would make them tough to beat. So he closely queried opposing coaches to see if they felt a youngster had the psychological makeup to play with a group.

The on-court sense of camaraderie that fans could sense whenever scoring Bruin players "thanked" the person who threw them the ball wasn't necessarily the result of our actually liking each other. They simply knew that this had to happen, or they would find themselves seated next to Coach so he could explain it to them. The 1963–64 undefeated championship team that was as cohesive as any UCLA team ever didn't get along very well off the court. There were only a couple of players on the squad who were popular with everyone, and a few were generally disliked by the rest of the squad. But when these Bruins hit the floor, those petty jealousies and interpersonal conflicts disappeared. Coach didn't demand that they be friends on their own time, but on the court they had to be teammates if they had any hope of playing.

Sometimes a remarkable young player would enroll at UCLA and hope that his quickness and athleticism would be so extraordinary that Coach would have to play him even though he played selfishly. Without exception, that young athlete would learn the hard way that the only way to get playing time was to fit in with the group. The best illustration of this is the story of one of the great UCLA players of all time, super-quick big man Sidney Wicks. I had played against Sidney when he was at Hamilton High School. At 6'8½" and about 235 pounds, Sidney had the strength of a power forward and the quickness of a point guard. He could fill the lane on the fast break as well as any player I ever saw. After playing his freshman year at Santa Monica College, Sidney arrived at UCLA ready to make a big splash.

The Bruins already had a pretty fair big man in Kareem Abdul-Jabbar, so it wasn't like there was no one else on the team. But Sidney was a major talent, he knew it, and he wanted the ball *now*. He was impatient, and he played a bit out of control. Rather than taking his time and letting the game come to him, Sidney made numerous mistakes trying to create a spectacular play. When Coach sat him down behind Lynn Shackelford, a senior who had marginal talent compared to Sidney, young Mr. Wicks was distraught and upset, and he went to Coach for an explanation of the obvious injustice. He asked Coach point-blank, "Aren't I a better player than Lynn Shackelford?" Without missing a beat, Wooden said, "Why yes, you are, Sidney, and when you learn to play *with* the team, you will start, but not before then." With Kareem leading the way, the Bruins easily rolled to the national championship with Wicks firmly planted on the bench in a backup role

Sidney was stubborn and had great pride, but he was also very smart. While it took Sidney his entire sophomore year to get the message, for the next two years he played team basketball under control. The improvement was absolutely startling. He not only became a reliable team player, he was named the National Player of the Year! Perhaps today a player of Sidney's physical talent would have just gotten fed up and transferred schools. But if John Wooden were still coaching, I suspect Sidney would have stayed. He was perceptive enough to know just how much better he would be coming out of the UCLA basketball program; if he had transferred, he never would have become the incredible impact player he ultimately was. But first he had to be convinced that teamwork was not an option, but a necessity.

It is vital for you to convey an appreciation of teamwork to people on every level of your organization. You cannot afford to concentrate all your attention on the top-level people, only to find that there are problems festering somewhere else in the organization. Coach Wooden understood that when the team lost, it would be easy for the people who didn't get in to feel that they weren't responsible or involved. It is no coincidence that though we only lost three times in my three years at UCLA—to Oregon, USC, and Notre Dame—Coach made it a point to get all the reserves in at the end of all three games. At the time, I thought it was sort of strange that Coach would put me in with little more than a minute left and these games too far out of reach to think a comeback was possible. But on reflection, I see how this strategy was brilliant. I came to UCLA to be a star, and star players expect to make big things happen; Coach depended on people like me to be arrogant enough to think we could have made a difference. So when the horn sounded and the loss was in the books, I felt as responsible for those losses as any guy in the room. How brilliant of Coach to understand that it's good to win as a team, but absolutely essential that you lose as a team. Because of this attitude, our post-loss players-only meetings were helpful, healing, and crucial to the eventual development of the powerful bonds that hold every successful team together. No one could stand at the back of the room and point fingers; we all had the chance to help the team win, and we all had failed.

Coach Wooden sold us all on the incredible possibilities that were attainable through team effort. Bill Walton described this beautifully when he told me, "He challenged us to believe that something special could come from the group effort. We live in a society that is constantly pushing us to be individual, to be selfish. But Coach Wooden constantly focused on the group, and how there could be no success unless everybody believed in the same goal and everybody came out of there feeling good about the success of others." That sense of team was perhaps the most important constant that Coach Wooden instilled throughout his coaching career.

In most organizations, every manager intrinsically understands that his various groups have to communicate well and work together. But far too often, managers don't understand that it is their job to make teamwork a must. Many talented people find working with others frustrating, so they simply decide that they'll work at their own pace and let the others be damned. You cannot allow this type of behavior. Teammates can cover your back, correct your mistakes, support you when you're down, and inspire you to do better. A cohesive group of people can actually defeat a far more talented compilation of individuals if the cohesive group sticks together. But you must know, as a manager, that insistence on teamwork will put you at odds with your most talented players. People with tremendous individual talent are always the toughest to convince about the importance of teamwork. But the only way to achieve tremendous success is to have talented individuals whom you mold into a team.

When I took over programming for the Channel One Network, the largest source of news and information for teenagers in America, there were deep divisions in our news department. People weren't communicating, deadlines were missed, harassment suits were everywhere, and teamwork was nonexistent. The first day I got there, I gathered everyone together to give them a sense of my expectations. First on my list was teamwork, which I considered an absolute necessity. I then went over, opened the door to the conference room, and invited anyone who wasn't willing to subvert their own agenda for the good of the group to please leave now—and I promised them that if they didn't leave now. they would be leaving in the weeks and months to come. Sure enough, by the end of the first year a large number of individuals had gone on to other employment—but they left a real team behind. Producers and reporters started sharing ideas, and encouragement and constructive criticism replaced yelling and backbiting. Meetings started on time, people met their deadlines, and the quality of the programming dramatically improved. This is where you need to stand tall as a manager, and be willing to go through tough times with some of your best people. Most people will ultimately fall into line and become team members, and those who don't will simply have to find work elsewhere.

Of course, one of the difficulties of insisting on teamwork is that often it's your most talented individuals who would rather not be a part of a team-oriented environment. They feel that because they're more talented, they have nothing to gain from working with others. I ran into this at Channel One, where my most talented producer was also resistant to the team concept. When I met with him to discuss this problem, I knew that he had to understand how strongly I valued teamwork. So after telling him how talented I thought he was, and how important he was to the success of the organization, I asked him to leave. He was clearly stunned. I told him that it looked to me like he would not or could not adapt to my system. By doing that, I left it up to him to assure me that he would change, rather than laying out my demands and having him merely nod his assent. The meeting was emotional and uncomfortable, but the result was that this brilliant producer really changed his ways. Honestly, I didn't think after our meeting that he would change, but I do know that the organization would have been better off without him if he wasn't capable of working with the group. And by getting him to convince me I was wrong, we created a much stronger "contract" for him to change his behavior.

This insistence on teamwork is one of the real secrets of the Pyramid, but it cannot be partially accomplished. There is nothing more destructive to an organization than a star player who makes a big contribution and then fails to acknowledge all the help he received, and there is nothing easier than that person praising the efforts of the co-workers who made a triumph possible. Praising others must become a habit on every level of your organization, not just the leadership. You must insist on this, and continue to make your expectations of teamwork clear, if you want to take your group—or have your group carry you—to the top.

RULES ARE MADE TO BE FOLLOWED, NOT BROKEN

ONE OF THE THINGS that set us apart from most college teams in the championship years is that punctuality and appearance were not negotiable. Imagine asking kids in 1970 to get short haircuts and remove their sideburns. There weren't another hundred people in the whole school who looked like we did. Every year, one of the top players would insist that they were not getting their hair cut. But when they were made to understand that *no one* was allowed into practice without an approved haircut, they all complied and toed the line. Punctuality was also a major issue, since most everyone who came to UCLA was the big star on their high school team, and they were used to having exceptions made for them. It didn't take long to realize that the rules applied to everyone, and there were consequences if they were broken. Coach also understood that if he expected us to be on time, we should not have to wait for him—and we never did.

But an equally important corollary to this is that it's important to limit the number of rules you impose on an organization. When John Wooden first started coaching, he had a lot of rules and a few suggestions. By the time he retired, he had a lot of suggestions and just a few rules. We recently discussed the prevalence of tattoos on today's youngsters, and I was not at all surprised to hear that Coach Wooden didn't like them at all. But he candidly admitted to me that despite his personal feelings, he wasn't sure he would refuse to recruit a tattooed player if he was still coaching today. This is tougher than forcing kids to get haircuts, since tattoos are pretty permanent, and many contemporary players already have them in high school. But knowing Coach as I do, I suspect that if he were still coaching, his team would be one of the only teams playing that was notable for its lack of tattoos.

Beyond rules about appearance and punctuality, the only other rules Coach enforced were that you were not allowed to criticize the play of a teammate, and that profanity was not allowed. Of course, you were also expected to attend classes and get passing grades, but this was never put down as a hard-and-fast rule. Naturally, players did use profanity on occasion, and the punishment was dismissal from practice. Many coaches would have punished this type of offense with some form of physical pain or discomfort in the form of extra running, but Coach viewed this as too negative and punitive. He knew that practice was when you got a chance to improve and earn more playing time, and throwing people out of practice proved far more effective than more obviously painful options.

Coach Wooden did not come to his principles late in his career; he was always willing to risk his won-lost record to some extent if it meant upholding team rules. While it's true that in all of his years of coaching, John

Wooden never had a losing record, he came awfully close to a losing season very early in his career. In his first year of coaching at basketball-mad South Bend (Indiana) Central High School, Coach had a crisis with his two best players that put his rules to the test. When the two stars did not show up for the team bus, Coach and the remaining players departed for the game against their crosstown rivals. Forced to play a couple of football players who had just joined the team, Coach Wooden's team fought their hearts out and won the game. The next day, Coach's wife, Nellie, saw the two absent players' pictures in the society page at a dance. That night, Coach and his wife had dinner with Mr. Pointer, the principal at South Bend Central, who had seen the boys' picture as well. Mr. Pointer asked young Coach Wooden how he was going to handle it, and Coach said he felt he needed to dismiss the boys from the team. A strong punishment to be sure, but Mr. Pointer supported his young coach. When Coach called both boys in to see him, they both lied and said they had missed the game because they were ill. Coach followed through on his word, and dismissed them from the squad. The pressure to reinstate them was tremendous, but Coach held his ground. His shorthanded team eked out a 14-12 record—and years later one of the boys he had dismissed saw Coach Wooden and thanked him for making him grow up. They might have won a few more games that year, but Coach got a reputation as a man of strong principles that served him well for decades to come.

Another early incident in Coach Wooden's career made him aware of the dangers of making the consequences for breaking a rule too hard-and-fast. While still at South Bend Central, Wooden instituted a rule that said if you were caught smoking you were automatically off the team. His most valuable player was caught smoking, and true to his word Coach summarily dismissed him from the squad. Not only did this dismissal cost his team a shot at the state title, but it had other consequences as well: The young man he dismissed from the squad quit school and dropped his plans to go on to college. From that time forward, he never stipulated what the punishment would be if a rule was broken. He believed that this case hadn't worked out well for his team or for the young man he'd disciplined, and he learned from it.

All organizations have rules; what tends to separate them is how those rules are applied. Many managers are afraid to impose strict rules because they're afraid of alienating their underlings. The first thing you accomplish by setting and enforcing rules is to positively reinforce those members of the group who would toe the line even if you didn't ask them to. Hopefully, your organization has a sizable group of solid citizens. Such employees are usually loath to complain when others get away with things, but the fact is, almost everyone hopes that the reckless guy who speeds through a red light gets caught and ticketed. You must support your "law-abiding citizens" by punishing persistent violators.

Coach Wooden's rule banning facial hair was something that he took very seriously. When Bill Walton decided to test the Coach on this and show up with a beard, he knew that as the premier player in the country he had a lot of clout. Coach asked Bill what was up with his beard, and Bill stated that he felt it was his right to have facial hair. Most coaches would have gotten extremely agitated at this type of confrontation, but not John Wooden.

He simply asked Bill if he felt strongly about this right to a beard, and Bill responded that he did indeed feel very strongly. Never raising his voice, Coach said, "Bill, I respect a man who has strong beliefs and is willing to stand up for them . . . and the team is going to miss you." No yelling, no ranting, just a strong and simple conversation. Not surprisingly, a shaven Bill Walton showed up for practice the next day!

But some rules manage to upset almost everyone in your organization (Coach Wooden's rules on hair length certainly did). So what do you do? If the rule covers something that is vitally important to you, stand by it. Your people will recognize the value of your integrity, and as a side benefit, their collective opposition can actually lead to a more cohesive team. Part of molding a great organization is the bonding that a group experiences when they're forced to do something that none of them wants to do. My absolute insistence on punctuality is rarely greeted with enthusiasm at first. I also insist that *all* phone calls must be returned within twenty-four hours. Not everything you do as an organization has to be fun and uplifting for it to have a positive effect. This presents problems for the leader who needs to be liked; if you feel a great need to always be popular with your charges, rules will be tough to impose. On the other hand, if you have enough confidence to focus on the long term, you'll find that imposing and carrying out rules will lead to a more cohesive team. You may find that over time your charges will respect you (and yes, even love you), even if they don't *like* you.

SECRET #17

CONCENTRATE ON **YOUR TEAM,** NOT THE OPPOSITION

THIS WAS TRULY one of Coach's great secrets—but it wasn't really much of a secret. He told *everyone* that he spent almost no time scouting other teams or running their plays in practice, but no one really believed him when he said it. Pretty strange for a man with such a great reputation for honesty to be doubted, but I think his fellow coaches all thought he was pulling their leg with this one. But everyone who played for UCLA has some great story about how little preparation we did for specific opponents. Of course, a few times a year the second string would run through an upcoming opponent's plays, and we would talk about tendencies and strengths. But before most games, Coach made almost no mention of the opponent during practice. His explanation for this is once again disarmingly simple, but the impact is complex.

First of all, there is a limited amount of practice time, and Coach felt if we did our job well, it really didn't matter who the opponent was or what tricks they had up their sleeve. The subliminal message is that we really believed that the outcome was firmly in our hands, not in the other team's. People always felt that UCLA teams seemed a bit cocky—and we were. While our opponents were spending countless valuable hours of practice time learning our plays and looking at film, we were concentrating solely on our own skills and team goals. We knew that with effort, execution, and focus, we would win.

How many companies have made awful decisions simply because "everyone else is doing it" seemed like a good enough reason at the time? It's still pretty hard to believe how many people got stuck in dot.com businesses that had no plan to make money at any time in the foreseeable future just because everyone else seemed to be riding such foolishness to higher and higher stock prices. Many executives who stressed fiscal responsibility and planning in 1998–99 were told that they "just don't get it," and that profits were a concept that no longer applied. The tech stock shakeout of the year 2000 suggests that a sound business model still matters in the long run. If you were confident enough to concentrate on what you knew, and continued to believe in the business principles you knew and understood, you were able to avoid the pitfall of believing that profits were no longer an applicable idea in the New Economy. It seems almost comical that this folly was accepted by many "experts" in so many businesses. Avoiding the temptation to study your opposition intently and to try to counter their every move takes maturity and confidence. Those also happen to be two key traits of natural leaders.

So many people in business are absolutely fixated on what their competition is doing. Industrial espionage is a multibillion-dollar business. But once again, what *you* believe in, and what *you* think your organization should be doing is what's important. There isn't enough time in the day to do your job and worry about the other guy, too. And the fact that "everyone else is doing it" doesn't mean it's the best way to go. My two biggest hits on network TV were both picked by the so-called experts to be the flops of the year when they debuted. Why? Simply because the shows were opposed to all the trends of the times. But that may be the biggest reason they worked. If we had focused on what other studios were doing, we never would have separated ourselves from the competition. Fortunately, we stuck with our game plan and ignored everyone else. So don't be afraid to buck the trends. Do what you do well, concentrate on getting your team to execute to the best of its ability, and trust that you'll be pleased with the outcome. Only a sucker spends so much time scouting the opponent that his own team can't play worth a lick.

SECRET #18

ADJUST TO YOUR PLAYERS—DON'T EXPECT THEM ALL TO ADJUST TO YOU

MANY LEADERS have developed a clear sense of how they like to do things, and they expect everyone in their organization to adapt to their style of management. For a person who might have seemed stuck in his ways, Coach Wooden was actually remarkably flexible when it came to the systems he employed and the ways he interacted with his young players. Lacking the ability to attract any great big men in the early 1960s, Coach was forced to find ways to utilize his team's quickness and great guard play with Walt Hazzard and Gail Goodrich; with strong input from Jerry Norman, his top assistant, Coach installed the full-court press to take advantage of his players' fast hands and great anticipation. His first national championship at UCLA in 1964 resulted from his accommodation to his centerless team. But when great centers like Kareem Abdul-Jabbar and Bill Walton were in tow, Coach changed his entire offensive set to take advantage of their low-post skills. Jamaal Wilkes had one of the strangest-looking jump shots that Coach had ever seen, but he never tried to change it because Jamaal could really shoot the ball. Henry Bibby had the odd habit of shooting his free throws from the far right-hand side of the line, but since he shot well over 80 percent, Coach never tried to make him change.

Coach also learned that though the players he coached in the 1950s would respond to "Jump!" by saying, "How high?" in the later years his players were more likely to ask "Why?" or "What for?" So long as Coach felt the question was being asked because the player really wanted to know, he always provided a quick and direct answer. His ability to adjust his teaching style is one of the key reasons he was able to win consistently over a long period of time with players of vastly different levels of talent. Though many people think that almost anyone could win with Kareem or Bill in the pivot (and even then they would be wrong), it is undeniable coaching greatness to win national championships with Fred Slaughter, Doug McIntosh, or Steve Patterson at the center spot.

Adjusting to your players also involves knowing who needs encouragement and who needs a kick in the rear end. Too many coaches adopt a single style of interaction with their players and expect them all to flourish. That simply doesn't take into account the basic fact of human nature that people are different. A coach needs to be a little bit like a jockey, and to adjust to the horse he's riding. Knowing what type of horse you're on is only half the battle; the other half is recognizing that you need to make the adjustments. Working with so many different people, Coach understood that he had to adjust his teaching style to fit the learner. Or as he put it, "Some players I had to pat on the back a lot . . . and then there were others that I had to pat a little lower, and a little harder." It is vital to point out here that not a single player that I spoke to felt that Coach had given them as much positive reinforcement as they would have liked. Though Coach feels that he was pretty positive as a rule, the truth is that he was exceedingly sparing in his praise. Maybe the players at UCLA would have been happier to get more loving support from Coach, but it is doubtful that this would have resulted in more effort or better teamwork. Constant praise loses its effectiveness; intermittent reinforcement keeps people hungry for more. A little bit of sugar actually goes further than a lot of it.

It takes a truly secure leader to understand that though they might want to kick an employee around the office for screwing up, they *must* consider what that person's value is to the organization, and what type of feedback they'll respond to the best. It doesn't matter what makes *you* feel better or more powerful; what matters is how you can get that person to change their behavior. An insecure leader constantly reminds his underlings who exactly is in charge. A secure leader knows that his leadership is not in question or being constantly challenged, which frees him to react both to the individual and the situation. But regardless of the individual player's psychological makeup, Coach understood that pride is a better motivator than fear. As Ken Heitz so aptly observed about the individualistic tendencies of talented ballplayers and highly paid professionals, "You can't lead cats with a cattle prod." Sounds like something Coach Wooden might say.

When I was running CBS Productions, I had a general rule that I expected script meetings with writers to run no longer than an hour and a half. It just seemed to me that most writers couldn't absorb more input than that, and much of what got communicated late in the meeting wasn't going to get integrated into the script. But every rule is made to be broken, and when we developed our first pilot script with the talented Martha Williamson (now executive producer of *Touched by an Angel*), it became clear that she wanted and responded well to long and expansive notes meetings. It wasn't unusual for our meetings with Martha to run for three or four hours, and to cover an incredibly diverse range of topics. Invariably, when she left the office, we would wonder whether the meeting had been productive; at times the discussions seemed tangential, amusing, and very personal, but quite disconnected from the project at hand. But when Martha's revisions arrived, we were always astonished to see the intricate and unexpected ways in which she had drawn the seemingly random threads of our lengthy conversation into her characters and story lines. Of course, it goes without saying that you only adjust your style when the individual in question is a major talent. Rules are made for the role players and the minor talents; superstars require that you adjust your style to suit theirs.

I once produced a television movie that starred the incredibly talented actress Faye Dunaway. Faye has probably appeared in as many outstanding movies as any living actor (*Chinatown, Bonnie and Clyde,* the original *Thomas Crown Affair, Network,* and *Three Days of the Condor,* to name a few) and she had a reputation for being pretty high-strung. As the executive producer, I was responsible for everything in the picture. Somehow, my presence on the set made her nervous. On the fourth day of production, she blew up and asked me to leave the set while she was working. Some people thrive on conflict, and it seemed clear she was looking for a fight. I waited until they were finished shooting the scene, and then I visited Faye in her dressing room. Rather than engage her in a shouting match, I simply told her that I was truly honored to know that a guy like me could actually make a star like her nervous. If her performance would be better without me on the set, I would be happy to leave. She was clearly surprised by my reaction; I'm pretty sure that most executive producers would have informed her that no one, including the star of the picture, was going to throw them off of *their* set. I felt it was better to adjust to her needs and leave my ego aside. Needless to say, within a few days she asked me why I was never on the set while she was working. I reminded her that she had asked me to leave, and she retracted the request. Far from seeing her as difficult and petulant, I thought it was pretty clear that she was insecure and scared; by demonstrating my confidence in her, I hoped that insecurity would diminish. Coach Wooden had taught me that certain players require you to adjust your own behavior rather than expecting them to get used to the way you like to do things.

SECRET #19

FAILING TO PREPARE IS
PREPARING TO FAIL

FAILING TO PREPARE IS PREPARING TO FAIL is another one of Coach's favorite sayings. Coach is a great believer in the value of repetition, and there was little chance of playing ball at UCLA without remembering this expression. Coach himself was the embodiment of this saying, because he was so thoroughly prepared for every practice he conducted. Coach spent literally hours every day deciding on the drills and sequence for each practice. When practice started and he reached into his pocket for that day's 3-by-5 card, we knew that his "lesson plan" was already committed to paper. Coach always arrived early for everything, since he knew that to be on time you had to give yourself a cushion. Besides, that way he could check to make sure the balls were in place, the floor was clean, and there would be no unanticipated problems. From how to put on your socks, to how to tie your shoes, to what to wear on the road, Coach made sure that we were fully prepared for everything. In fact, we were so well prepared that Coach made it his goal *never* to call timeout during a game. He'd done his work in practice, and he expected the players to fully execute once the game began. No doubt there were many times when it was tempting for him to stop play to give advice, but the confidence he projected by leaving the game to the players was invaluable. And that confidence was born of his absolute certainty that his team was properly prepared.

In businesses that rely on creativity for their success, the truly talented people are often the ones most inclined to shirk preparation and try to rely on their improvisational skills in the workplace. The same is true in basketball, where the great individual talents always love to freelance and work on their own. No need to commit a pitch to paper, or to learn the plays the coach wants to run; the star talent often enjoys the thrill of making it up on the spot. Many talented individuals have gotten by without preparing simply because they were smarter, or faster, or more articulate, or taller. In each case, the manager's or coach's job is to insist on adequate preparation regardless of talent level. Sometimes untalented teams can overcome much more talented opponents as a result of outstanding preparation and execution. And the truly talented *and* prepared team is virtually impossible to beat. Ken Heitz, a key player on three NCAA championship teams at UCLA, is, as I've mentioned, now a co-managing partner at one of the top law firms in Los Angeles. He credits the lessons he learned about the value of preparation from John Wooden as the key to his success in high-stakes litigation work; in both basketball and the law, it's what you do before the spotlight hits the court that makes the difference.

Even just deciding how to prepare has a hidden value:

The manager who is committed to the value of preparation is forced to look honestly at the weaknesses and faults of the team, focus on the goals and dreams of the organization, and formulate a plan of attack that will allow them to reach those goals. Improvisation is valuable only within the boundaries and direction that the leader has outlined. When workers know their boundaries, have developed the skills they need to achieve their tasks, and are prepared for different eventualities and outcomes, some improvised strokes of genius can then push you to new heights. But preparation is the key to making sure that everyone in your organization is on the same page, working toward the same goals. Failing to prepare is preparing to fail.

Make sure the people on your team have a chance to meet and discuss their opinions *before* you meet with others involved in the project. As I've described, I made it a point always to meet with my creative executives to discuss their notes on a script before the writer came in, so we could hash out our differences in private; it wasn't that I minded disagreements, but I did want us to present a cohesive and united front. The time for us to disagree was in the preparation phase, not in the actual creative meeting. Getting together ahead of time to discuss a script gave everyone a chance to express ideas and float potential revisions in a collegial atmosphere. But at the breakneck pace of most businesses these days, it is precisely these sorts of planning and discussion meetings that fall by the wayside. Far too many managers spend all their time dealing with crises, tending to what seems more important now while letting the everyday business take care of itself. But preparation and planning *are* truly important, and if you commit the time you need to be prepared, you'll find that you have far fewer crises to manage. The manager who ignores the need to plan will always have so many fires to put out that he'll be convinced there is no time for anything else. Creating time for preparation and organization is the real key to organizational efficiency.

SECRET #20

PRACTICE DOESN'T MAKE PERFECT; ONLY *PERFECT* PRACTICE MAKES PERFECT

FOR A MAN with so many bromides, Coach was surprisingly sharp in pointing out the common sayings that made no sense to him. If you asked Coach if he thought a player had given 110 percent effort, he would give you a pretty cutting and sarcastic response. He felt the same way about "Practice makes perfect." In truth, practicing bad habits simply makes it more likely that you'll repeat those bad habits in a game. Coach was insistent on repetition, and it's clearly one of the keys to learning. But you must repeat the desired behavior only. As Coach often said, "You will play like you practice." So shoddy work habits and careless mistakes were never tolerated at any time. Perhaps surprisingly at the age of ninety, John Wooden doesn't miss coaching the games, recruiting, being in the media spotlight, or winning national championships. The only thing he misses is practice.

Coach was an absolute stickler for attention to detail and consistency, and this applied to practice as well as games. When I played ball in college, dunking was illegal. Asking talented, young, high-flying players like Sidney

Wicks, Bill Walton, or Larry Farmer never to dunk is a tall order, but since that was the rule in games, that was the rule in practice. Every once in a while, when Coach had his back turned, someone would throw down a slam—but no one ever did it when they thought that Coach was watching. When he would occasionally leave practice to let his top assistants run the show, it was never long before someone would dunk just to be rebellious. More often than not, they would shortly find out that Coach hadn't left the building; he was just sitting up high in the rafters to watch from a different perspective. Nothing escaped his attention. On the fast break, we were told to *never* throw crosscourt passes, and always to pull up at the free throw line. When a player would make a successful cross-court pass, he would sometimes be surprised by the chewing-out that followed. But Coach knew that championship-level teams would intercept those passes, and he was preparing us to beat the best, not the also-rans. If repetition is one of the four keys to teaching and learning, then repetition of mistakes is worse than harmless; it's deadly.

In a business environment, most employees are not fond of rehearsals and pre-meetings. They seem phony, almost a waste of time. But running through a sales pitch before your big meeting will be effective—provided you turn off the phones, insist on no interruptions, and go through the pitch exactly as you would with a client in the room. Repetition is a key to successful execution, and you must be willing to simulate "game" conditions and deliver a peak performance. Rehearsal presentations that are filled with pauses, confusing sentences, missing slides, and vague promises like "I'll be ready tomorrow" are simply inexcusable. Your role as a leader is to make your expectations crystal clear and not tolerate excuses. The kid whose dog ate his homework in junior high is the same person who shows up at your presentation run-through without notes. These people must either change their behavior or leave the organization. There is no doubt that Coach is right that *only perfect practice makes perfect.*

SECRET #21

BE HONEST, DIRECT, AND WILLING TO *RISK IT ALL* FOR YOUR BELIEFS

WHAT DO YOU DO if the best player in the country doesn't want to cut his hair and practice is about to start? If you're John Wooden, you make sure there's an empty chair at the barbershop and that the player clearly understands that without a haircut he cannot be a member of the team. Is it really worth it to risk a national championship over a haircut? Without a doubt! In fact, I'm sure Coach would say we never would have won a single national championship without those haircuts . . . and thirty years later I'm beginning to think he's right. Coach had a very clear idea of what he wanted to do and very little tolerance for those individuals who resisted his concepts; this was obvious to everyone in the program. We all knew that he had his core beliefs that would not be compromised for anyone on the team, regardless of stature. While an All-American might get away with being late or some other minor infraction, there is no doubt that a serious breach of Coach Wooden's rules would have resulted in expulsion for any player in the program.

Early in my career in Hollywood, I was in charge of movies and miniseries for Columbia Pictures Television. One of the first projects we got going was a four-hour picture on the life of Anwar Sadat. We shot the picture in Mexico at over eighty locations in a little more than forty days, almost impossible under the best of circumstances. The producers had hired a talented yet temperamental Dutch director of photography. He fought with the crew, he was demanding of everyone, but the film looked incredible. As we struggled to make our impossible schedule, my bosses at the studio decided the cameraman was a problem and had to be fired. I knew this fellow was an amazing artist, so I saw it as my job to make sure he stayed on the picture. I remember one Sunday getting paged on the tennis court to take a call from my irate boss asking me why this fellow hadn't been fired yet. As I argued vehemently to save this guy's job, the cameraman's agent (who happened to be one of the guys in our doubles game) walked off the court in frustration with my absence. But my passion for this man's talent paid off, he stayed on the picture, and he did an amazing job. Today, this director of photography, Jan de Bont, is one of the top directors in Hollywood, with films like *Speed* and *Twister* to his credit. When you know you are right, you must be willing to take risks to back your judgment.

I have a similar story from my days at CBS, where I really put this theory to the test. We were producing *Walker, Texas Ranger,* starring martial arts champion–action star Chuck Norris. Midway through the first full season, enormous problems started to develop between Chuck and the man who was executive-producing the series. Chuck wanted him fired, but my boss at CBS wanted the producer kept on at all costs. Chuck's manager begged me to fly down to Dallas to meet with Chuck to see if I could solve this seemingly impossible situation. I hopped a plane to Dallas with some of the most recent scripts that Chuck hated, and four hours later I was on the ground in Texas. By the time I reached Chuck's trailer, I had finished reading all the scripts, and had to agree with Chuck that they really weren't very good—but I had no idea how to solve this problem. I barely knew Chuck, I knew my boss did not want to make a change, and I was afraid that Chuck would walk off a hit show if we didn't make a change. There was one other disturbing piece of information that I thought about as I climbed the stairs into Mr. Norris's trailer: I was about to have a tough meeting with a guy who could actually kill me with his bare hands if he didn't like my answers. Now that's pressure.

I exchanged a few minutes of pleasantries with Chuck. He's a former world karate champion, as much an athlete as he is an actor, so I gave him a brief rundown of my athletic career at UCLA, which I could tell he found impressive. (So one of us did, anyway.) We at least established some common ground before the tough part of the meeting got going. He then launched into his speech voicing his concerns. His intensity burned bright as he rattled off his concerns and demands: He hates the executive producer, he doesn't want to work with him, if the producer isn't replaced, Chuck will not return for the next season, Chuck wants to be named the new executive producer. Now I happened to agree with Chuck that we needed a new producer, but I thought the idea of Chuck taking over was unrealistic. Heck, he was already working about fifteen hours a day; he'd have to work 24/7 to take over the whole show. Besides, I really liked my boss at CBS, and my boss had made it clear that the executive producer was not to be fired. How could I ever hope to get out of this mess? I looked at Chuck to make sure he was finished talking (never interrupt a man who is lethal), and then I asked him when the next flight out of Dallas was taking off. He told me, and I asked him to send for the car. I was obviously not in a position to help him out. Chuck was confused, as he thought I agreed with him about the current producer. I told him that I did agree with him, I just didn't think that the solution was to replace the old producer with the star of the show. I told Chuck that he seemed like a real nice guy, but that I wasn't going to lie to him and tell him I would help if I didn't approve of his plan. Chuck looked me in the eye for what felt like ten minutes, and then asked me if I would be willing to help him get a new producer if he didn't ask for the job himself. I told him absolutely, although I couldn't guarantee we'd be successful. He was so taken aback that someone would actually risk telling him the truth that he agreed to work with me to try and effect a change. I had risked the fate of the entire series, but felt I had no choice. After much lobbying and hard work, we did make the change, and the series is still running strong years later. You have to be willing to put it all on the line if you hope to win big!

NOW you've had the opportunity to get a firsthand look at the "secrets" that made John Wooden the greatest coach of the twentieth century. Study them, make them the foundation of how you manage your team, and you will immediately become a vastly improved and more successful leader. No doubt, some managers are just more naturally gifted than other managers; John Wooden was a greatly talented manager. Since there is no handy formula that says "combine two parts quickness with three parts balance" to guide the application of these ideas, your natural instincts and talents will dictate how well you can integrate Coach Wooden's style into your own. But if you're willing to make some mistakes, continue to be quick without hurrying, and keep your balance at all times, your growth and success as a manager will be astonishing.

III

ME AND COACH

IN A SOCIETY where people constantly change to keep up with the times, John Wooden stands out because he has so little personal need to keep up or fit in. Los Angeles is a show-biz town; people hug people they just met, kiss people they hardly know, and consider anyone they've shared a meal with a friend. But Coach is still a Hoosier, despite the fact that he's lived in Los Angeles since 1948. Coach is not a highly demonstrative man, and he certainly doesn't wear his emotions on his sleeve. Yet, as with any successful teacher, his students were all desperate for his somewhat sparing approval. Every Bruin player fought hard for playing time, hoping for the chance to get in the game and hit a big shot. The payoff was seeing Coach show his pleasure in your performance with a quick smile, a short comment of approval, or just an enthusiastic fist pump with his rolled-up program. But as I reconnected with Coach in my late forties, I knew I had no heroic jump shots left in me, and though I thought that he had actually come to like me, I wasn't really sure.

One day I left Coach a couple of tapes of programs I

had produced, hoping he would watch them and knowing he would love to see the positive values these shows celebrated. Just a couple of days later he returned the tapes, along with a short note of appreciation. I folded the note in my pocket and forgot about it for a few days. Then, in a meeting with a fellow I worked with who was a big hoops fan, I remembered this note and thought he would enjoy seeing it. I fumbled through my pockets and unfolded the letter. He read it, looked at me, and said, "Wow, this is amazing." It was a nice note from my quick reading, but amazing? He handed it back to me and I read it again; on my second reading, I saw the closing that Coach had used. It was signed, "Love, Coach." This was better than "nice shot." I went out that day and got that folded letter framed. It hangs proudly on my office wall. And it leaves me a little sad that I spent nearly twenty-five years shutting Coach out of my adult life.

Some of Coach Wooden's former players were lucky enough to maintain a close relationship with him throughout their post-college years. For some of them, he has been influential in ways that are immeasurable. One man who has been blessed with Coach's counsel and wisdom as he's grown and matured is my old teammate John Vallely. An All-American at UCLA, John was drafted in the first round of the 1970 NBA draft by the Atlanta Hawks. Making plans to leave for Atlanta, John asked his girlfriend Karen to join him. But Karen balked since no marriage proposal was forthcoming, and John was in a real quandary. He turned to Coach Wooden for advice. Coach told him in no uncertain terms that he should "marry that girl." Fortunately, for John Vallely, he listened to Coach, and he and Karen got married before they left for Atlanta. Coach Wooden's advice continued to play a big role in their lives in the years that followed.

After John's short career in the pros, the two moved back to Newport Beach to settle down with their young family. John Vallely is one former UCLA player who was forced to put the life skills he learned under Coach Wooden to perhaps the ultimate test. Vallely was a tremendous college player who was at his best in big games and under great pressure; his ability to stay focused and put forth his best effort gained him the respect of all his teammates. When John and Karen learned that their nine-year-old daughter, Erin, had cancer, they were forced to draw upon all the lessons that Coach Wooden had ever imparted. Perhaps no lesson was as valuable as understanding that as a player, as in life, you can only focus on your own effort, not the ultimate outcome. Their fight with cancer on behalf of their daughter was far tougher than any basketball game, and longer than any season. It tested their strength and resolve in ways that are hard to imagine. But their story is an incredible example of how important it is to concentrate on the things that are under your control, and to strive for the peace of mind that comes not from victory, but from knowing that you've done your very best.

John was an active and involved father, coaching his daughter's soccer team, when she told him that she didn't feel well and her stomach hurt. Within a matter of days they were hit with the diagnosis of cancer, and little Erin underwent her first of many operations, this one to remove a cantaloupe-sized tumor. As John pointed out to me, most marriages cannot withstand the horrible pressures and strains of having a child with a serious illness; he and Karen knew they had to pull together with a maximum effort to make sure their marriage stayed strong and that they did absolutely everything in their power to help their girl recover from this dread disease. They poured their heart and soul into her recovery, and after two and a half years, the doctors believed that Erin was in sight of a full recovery. But then the Vallelys received a devastating setback when a family vacation in Palm Springs was cut short by the sudden excruciating pains that Erin was having in her abdomen. They rushed back to the hospital, where another tumor was found in their girl. How does a couple keep going when faced with seemingly insurmountable odds? John knew he needed to stay intent on the effort that he and Karen made every day. They could not start to crumble as the chances of recovery started to fade. Every day, getting on the elevator at the hospital, John would recall the lessons he had learned from Coach Wooden, and prayed for the strength to keep going, to make the maximum effort each day to make that day as positive as it could be for his family. They worked with the doctors in the hopes of finding a chemotherapy treatment that would halt this awful disease.

Tragically, Erin Vallely died when she was twelve years old. Over a thousand people attended her memorial service. John and Karen had done absolutely everything a couple could do to help their daughter recover, and some people might mistakenly say that they had failed. But they knew in their hearts that they had made an amazing effort, and had simply received an outcome that was hard to accept. But they were able to accept their fate because they knew they had left nothing undone or unsaid. Their marriage had survived, and emerged even stronger than before. As John told me, "Life isn't all about winning every event that we enter." Coach Wooden used to say that we should "hold our heads high" after a loss, that losing was not a terrible indignity but a part of life. John and Karen have taken these lessons from the basketball court and applied them to the most difficult test that life can offer. They surely can hold their heads high. They are justifiably proud to have beaten the odds and recently celebrated their thirtieth wedding anniversary. John Vallely learned from John Wooden that peace of mind is the goal to strive for in life. I sure consider John Vallely to be one of the most successful men I know.

IN SOME WAYS, it seems strange to me to feel so close to Coach Wooden, who for many years of my life I had viewed as a teacher who had failed me in his class for three straight years. Though many of Coach's former players are in contact with him, I suspect there are still many who feel like I did before I took the time to get to know him as an adult. Part of what contributed to these unpleasant feelings was that when you were playing for Coach Wooden, virtually everyone you spoke to about him assumed that he was as sweet and gentle as their favorite grandfather. No one wanted to hear that he had disappointed you in any way, or that he was less than perfect. But as an adult, I've found it emotionally cathartic to learn that one person who knows that John Wooden was not perfect is Coach himself. The first time I saw this side of him, it really stunned me. We were discussing the qualities that every good leader must possess. Reaching into a stack of papers, he pulled out a list he had prepared for a speech he made years ago. How he knows where all this stuff is hidden is a mystery to me, but he knows exactly where he has left every note, every letter, every photograph. He went down his list, and I nodded in agreement with everything he said. But when he got to the point where he stated that a good leader must make every effort to praise those who are not in the spotlight, since the people out of the spotlight don't get approval from external sources, I was in a quandary. Should I nod in agreement, or speak up? I remembered how many times I had desperately needed Coach to pat me on the back, a gesture that never came. But I had no desire to argue with Coach, and I knew that he truly believed he had done this successfully. Still, quietly, hopefully, and I hoped respectfully, I decided to interrupt Coach and let him know that as someone who spent three years on his bench, this was an area in which he had not followed his own precepts. Much to my surprise, Coach neither bristled with antagonism nor argued with my response; he simply admitted that I was probably right, he had made mistakes like anyone else, and that he wished he had done better. Oddly enough, this admission was a cathartic moment for me. Simply and plainly, Coach had admitted his own fallibility and humanity. How could I continue to harbor any feelings of anger and resentment? The moment passed quickly, but its impact went deep.

In May of 1999 I went to my first UCLA basketball reunion in over a decade. It was a big event with well over a hundred former players and their wives. A packed room, and yet no one there had played ball when I was in school. Now, reunions like this had never been my favorite thing anyhow; they always brought back memories of sitting on the bench until the final minutes of the game. I had gotten past that feeling when I was sitting with Coach in his den, but being in the company of all these old ballplayers rekindled my old insecurities. In fact, as I stood in the hallway outside the banquet hall, I momentarily thought about just going back to my car and leaving. I asked the organizer, a former player, if any of the guys from my era were expected, and he said "No—but why don't you sit over there next to Coach?" "You bet," I responded, and as I walked across the room, I thought about how totally unlikely my sitting with Coach would have been just a short time ago. But sit with him I did, and all night long he took great paternal pride in telling all who came by our table that "Andy works in television, and he worked on that wonderful program *Touched by an Angel!*"

All those years of hoping for Coach's approval, and now I was getting it in a way I never could have imagined. We seemed to agree about almost nothing when I was playing for him; now we agreed about virtually everything. It felt awfully good. And then, after dinner was served, something extraordinary happened that I will never forget. Coach is from Indiana, where men show affection by a smile, and maybe a handshake. But while old players gave speeches and told jokes, I suddenly felt Coach's hand on top of mine. This man had seemed so totally distant and unreachable, and here he was holding my hand. After a couple of minutes, he removed his hand. No words were exchanged. None had to be.

Then, in March of 2000, I had one of my regular breakfasts with Coach and his son-in-law, Dick. We talked about sports, politics, and old players we had known. Coach told a few stories about his early days at UCLA, when he had to mop the gym floor himself before practice. Then we went back to his apartment to talk some more. He showed me a book of photographs given to him by one of his great-granddaughters. Sitting in this room filled to bursting with awards, trophies, and priceless photographs, Coach told me that this photo book is the greatest gift he has ever received. His joy was palpable, and it was wonderful to share it with him. While I was thumbing through this prized possession, the phone rang. I continued to look at the pictures, drawings, and inventive captions, while his answering machine finished the familiar "please speak slowly and distinctly" and then beeped.

The voice on the other end belonged to a Southern gentleman, and after a few words Coach leaned over and picked up the call. He chatted amiably with this man, briefly thanked him, and was off the phone. He immediately turned his attention to what I thought of his treasured book; I expressed my admiration for the love and caring that this book of pictures represents. Since he often receives phone calls from people I know, I asked him about the call he just received. Coach replied, "Oh, that was a man from the Atlanta Athletic Club. They have just voted me the Coach of the Century." Just like that, oh by the way . . . he was just named the Coach of the Century. Not wanting to dwell on his own honor too long, he immediately added that I would be happy to know that UCLA is well represented, "because Lewis [Kareem Abdul-Jabbar] was named the Player of the Century." No doubt about it, he was more excited about Kareem's selection than his own. And he was far more excited about his great-granddaughter's precious gift.

When it was time to go, I told Coach to sit still and I

would see myself out. He wouldn't hear of it, and insisted on seeing me to the elevator as he always does. He can barely walk, but that's not the point. Coach is stubborn, that's for sure. The elevator arrived, and I stuck out my hand for a goodbye handshake. To my utter shock and amazement, Coach ignored my hand and embraced me in a warm hug. I knew that if I didn't get out of there fast, I might actually start to cry. In the alley outside his condo, I sat in my car for some time, alone with my feelings. I now knew that I had his love and respect, and this knowledge was beyond price. He is a great man, and I am privileged to know him.

Spending time reconnecting with John Wooden has been one of the most deeply satisfying and rewarding experiences of my life. I've had the opportunity to take my sense of bitter disappointment and resentment, and replace it with a sense of accomplishment and gratitude—a wonderful trade-off. And writing this book with him has given me the perfect excuse to see him regularly and get to know him in a way that I never thought possible. The mentor relationship is a very powerful one; so is the soul-satisfying completeness of reconnecting and getting to say a proper thank-you. But there have been some other recent and unexpected joys that have come out of this renewed relationship with Coach Wooden, further proof that the best things in life are not material goods but emotional ones.

The first involves my dear friend and high school coach, Courtney Borio. Courtney was a seldom-used reserve on the UCLA teams in the early 1950s, and his coaching style incorporated much of what he learned from John Wooden. But like many players, he had little contact with Wooden after graduation. It wasn't that Courtney didn't hold Wooden in the highest regard, but he felt awkward making contact. Courtney did send a number of his University High School players on to Westwood, but none of them had great success on the court. I'm sure Courtney always felt a little guilty, that perhaps he should have recommended his players go somewhere other than UCLA to pursue their dreams. Over the years, Coach Borio and Coach Wooden lost touch and didn't speak for some time. While my relationship with John Wooden in my first two decades after college can safely be described as almost nonexistent, my old high school coach and his wonderful, warm, and courageous wife, Linda, became like parents or older siblings to my wife and me. Where John Wooden had not been the father figure I hoped he would or could be for me, Courtney Borio was all that and more. But the wheel of life keeps turning, and eventually it was my turn to support my pal Courtney, as his beloved Linda succumbed to the final stages of a thirty-year battle with cancer.

Like John Wooden, Courtney had met his sweetheart in high school and had the type of marriage that results from two people who know they are with the only person they will ever want to love for the whole of their lives. Coach Wooden speaks often of his enduring love for his departed wife, Nellie; he still writes her a love letter on the twenty-first of every month to honor her birthday. I am lucky enough to have the same sort of marriage to my wife, Janice, that both of my coaches had with their departed spouses. But a loss of this magnitude can often leave the surviving spouse in a state of depression and disbelief. Fortunately, I knew that if anyone could understand what Courtney was going through it was Coach Wooden. Before Linda passed away, she spoke often of her desire to attend my fiftieth birthday party, which was scheduled for the middle of July. Sadly, she passed away two months before the party. But she definitely would have wanted Courtney to attend without her. The trouble was, my friend Courtney was so depressed that attending a party, even for his friend and former student, seemed to be more than he could bear. So I hatched a plan.

Bringing my relationship with John Wooden full circle was something that meant a lot to me, so I invited him to my fiftieth birthday bash. Coach isn't much for parties, but he accepted the invitation and joined with me in my plan. I knew that if I gave Courtney a job to do he would do it, so I made Courtney responsible for picking up Coach Wooden and bringing him to the party. It's not that Coach Wooden doesn't drive anymore; he is proud to point out that he has logged over twenty thousand miles on his 1989 Taurus, but a ride from a former player is always appreciated. Courtney hadn't spent any real time with John Wooden in nearly forty years, but he immediately sparked to my idea and agreed to do it. I knew that Linda would be thrilled that Courtney would not be missing the party.

The day before the party, I got a really big shock in the form of a surprise visit from my old teammate John Ecker. I was both thrilled and stunned to see him, since John had moved to Germany after college and had lived there ever since. Like many of my old teammates, John still harbored some uncomfortable feelings about his years at UCLA, and he had totally lost touch with John Wooden. After I recovered from the thrill of seeing my old basketball pal, I grew anxious about what John would think about our old nemesis John Wooden coming to my birthday party. Would he think I was a sellout, a hypocrite, an opportunist, or what? But I knew that John Ecker would love to see Coach Borio, who had been his high school coach, too. Maybe, just maybe, things would go okay with Coach Wooden, too. We were planning to have over a hundred guests at our party, but I was only nervous about John Ecker and his feelings toward Coach Wooden.

The night of the party rolled around, and my head was spinning with greeting guests and last-minute arrangements. With the party set for seven o'clock, I knew from years of experience that Coach Wooden would be precisely on time. Sure enough, at the appointed hour, Courtney, his son Mike, and Coach Wooden arrived. I was thrilled and moved that they were there to celebrate with me. Courtney and I briefly reflected on how much Linda would have loved to be there, but how proud she would be that Courtney somehow found the strength to come. I got Coach Wooden settled in a comfortable chair, and then went looking for John Ecker. I found him a few minutes later and asked him when he was going to say hello to Coach Wooden, and as I feared, John wasn't really sure he wanted to. So many years had passed, so many feelings repressed, and he just didn't want to bring it all back to the surface. But he's a good friend and a considerate guy, so he came with me to greet his old coach. They hadn't spoken in nearly twenty years.

Fortunately, I had my camera ready as the 6'7" Ecker embraced the much smaller Coach Wooden. We took a few pictures together, and then I left John and Coach seated together and hoped they would spend some time and catch up. Maybe it was because it was my birthday, but I got my wish: They spent much of the night catching up on old times. Very satisfying.

It was a fantastic party. Near the end of the evening, some close friends made some highly complimentary toasts that I found touching. Obviously, they were too touching for some, so my pal Bill Walton shouted out from the back of the crowd, "Hey, slow down, he's not dead yet!" The laughter and warmth were all I could hope for as I started my second half-century.

The morning after the party, we were all still buzzing with the excitement of the evening. It couldn't have gone better. Courtney had been there, as Linda would have hoped. Coach Wooden was there, as I had hoped. John Ecker had finally left his feelings of discomfort behind. I immediately got the pictures developed, and when I showed John Ecker the picture of Coach Wooden hugging him he stared at it for what seemed like an hour. He shook his head in amazement and said, "From this picture you'd think he was really happy to see me." Of course, the truth is, John Wooden was moved and excited to see his now-grown, mature, and successful former student. Ecker had a hard time believing that at first, but gradually, and slowly, he started to accept the fact that his old coach truly and deeply liked him. He came to realize that he had spent the past thirty years in denial, thinking that John Wooden's approval was neither necessary nor important. He had to admit that it felt really good to know that Coach really did have a soft spot in his heart for John Ecker.

That morning at the breakfast table, I knew that John finally would start feeling the sense of accomplishment about his college experiences that he had denied himself for his entire adult life. His career at UCLA, far from being years spent pursuing a goal he hadn't reached, were in fact one of the greatest achievements of his life outside of the beautiful family he has created. He had played a role in history. As I said to John, "Here we are, two of only thirteen guys in history to play on three NCAA championship teams . . . and I'll be damned if we shouldn't both be thrilled about that." Slowly and inexorably, with an occasional glance back at the picture of his warm hug with Coach, John started to share in the feelings that I had been rediscovering ever since I had picked up the phone to thank my old adversary for all he'd done for me. It was as if John was removing an emotional rock from his shoe, one he'd walked around with for so many years that he had almost convinced himself that it didn't hurt. But once removed, the sensation of feeling no pain was unimaginably liberating; replacing that pain with warm and positive feelings is indescribable.

What is the greatest gift a man could get on his birthday? For me, it was the knowledge that John Wooden was my friend; that I had helped my old high school coach, Courtney Borio, on the road to recovery after his devastating loss; and that my sidekick John Ecker could now look back and reflect on his athletic accomplishments with a sense of pride and satisfaction that he had denied himself for over thirty years. As Ralph Waldo Emerson said (and Coach Wooden is fond of quoting), "It is one of the most beautiful compensations of this life that no man can sincerely help another without helping himself." How right he was.

John Ecker sent me a copy of the letter he wrote to

Coach shortly after returning to Germany. Reading it was warmly satisfying for me. Perhaps you'll see why:

Dear Coach Wooden:

I wanted to take the time to say how much I enjoyed seeing you at Andy's birthday party. As you well know, I wasn't really sure of your true feelings about me during my years at UCLA. I have always had the greatest respect for you as a person and for your unbelievable accomplishments as a basketball coach. To this day I remain in awe of you. Your knees may not work very well anymore (age is not always kind to the joints of former basketball players!), but your mind is still incredibly sharp. When I look in the mirror, there's no mistaking the signs of a senior citizen. But while talking to you, I felt as if time had somehow passed you by without taking its usual toll. Above all, I felt closeness to you that I had never felt before, perhaps because I had always feared you a little bit and had been afraid to approach you. Chatting so easily with you that evening gave me the distinct and pleasurable feeling of talking to a member of my family with whom I had been happily reunited after a long period of absence. I will remember those special moments with you at Andy's house for a very long time.

Thanks for a wonderful evening. I wish you all my best and pray that your knees don't cause you too many problems. I'll make a point of dropping by when I come to Los Angeles next; I don't intend to wait another twenty years to see you again!

Your friend and admirer,
John Ecker

As Coach is fond of saying, "Love is the greatest of all words in our language." In my twenties, Coach Wooden had seemed to me to be a provincial and anachronistic man. Now he seems so insightful and cutting-edge. He hasn't changed much, but I have . . . and I do love him. As he is fond of saying, "It is what you learn after you know it all that counts."

AFTERWORD
BY JOHN WOODEN

I T IS DIFFICULT for people to understand and accept a "back seat" in a program of a type in which they had formerly starred at another level, and that was precisely the position in which Andy Hill found himself when he entered UCLA. However, he endured the situation and graduated with honors, which is far more important than his role on an athletic team. In team participation there are different roles to be filled, and while Andy did not get the role he preferred, he persevered and played an important part in three consecutive NCAA championship basketball teams. It is also clear from working with Andy on this book that he fully integrated the lessons we tried to teach on the hardwood into his business and personal life. In fact, Andy points out areas of my teachings that I was even not aware of, and in so doing created a relationship with me that is very gratifying.

I am most proud of the fact that almost all of my players at UCLA graduated and received degrees. They have done well, many exceptionally well, in whatever profession they chose to pursue. The fact that many became attorneys, teachers, doctors, dentists, businessmen, and coaches, among other professions, indicates that the lessons they learned about working together have helped them reach success regardless of their tremendous diversity of individual skills.

Since I firmly believe that the youth of today need role models more than critics, I like to feel that the devotion I have had to my wife and family had some influence on the fact that so many of those under my supervision have gone on to create wonderful marriages and families of their own. Family, faith, and friends are the cornerstones of a happy and fulfilling life.

Thank you, Andy, for capturing the essence of what I tried to get across in the classroom as well as in sports. If the teachings in this book can help you achieve success and fulfillment in your own life, that knowledge would please me very much.

ACKNOWLEDGMENTS

To John Wooden, Courtney Borio, and Gary Cunning-ham, who taught me so much about leadership, life, and balance. Thank you.

To every one of my fellow Bruin teammates who shared their insights and experiences with me, please accept my deepest appreciation. In particular, John Ecker, Bill Walton, and John Vallely; their open and affirmative enthusiasm for this project was a powerful source of positive energy.

To my wife, Janice; my kids, Alexandra and Aaron; and my entire, amazing extended family (most especially Rick and Claude), my heartfelt gratitude. Your collective love, support, loyalty, and good karma make life worth living.

To my many treasured and trusted friends who confidently insisted that I write this book, my hope that your confidence has been rewarded. Dan Blatt, Fred Barron, Miki Lane, Susan Tick, Steve Warner, Chris Barrett, Layne Britton, John and Barbara Rosove, Rick Rosen, Scott Garen, Glenn Adilman, Kelly Goode, Kevin Stein, Joe Richland, Dan Richland, Larry Lyttle, Tim O'Donnell, Laurie Levit, Steve Ades, Harry Thomason, Jeff Ballabon, Paul Folkemer, Rod Perth, Dan Strouse, Brian Lowry, Bill Kane, Ed Palmer, Leon Brachman, Bob Rehme, Dan Fellman, Ken Ross, Joel Fields, Ed Dawson, and Hoover Wilder . . . not one of you questioned whether I could actually write a book. You just assumed I could. What the heck were you thinking?

To my agents, Christy Fletcher and Chris Silbermann, for their insightful guidance and endless encouragement, and my lawyer, Bob Harris, for being so reachable and responsive, I am much obliged. To Lisa Temple Brunner for her tireless transcription typing.

To my talented editor at Simon & Schuster, Jeff Neuman, for helping me realize my vision, I wish for him a lifetime filled with fairways and greens.

To Jeff Sagansky, Jonathon Axelrod, and Michael Jaffe, who all gave me opportunities to grow and succeed in the entertainment business. Everyone needs someone to take a chance on them, and I am lucky to have had three people go out on a limb for me.

To the countless mentors, teachers, leaders, and coaches who have consciously modeled themselves on Coach John Wooden, since I know your impact has been positive and profound, I salute you.

And finally, to those of you who I hope now feel inspired and prepared to emulate Coach, my very best wishes. You have chosen a worthy goal. Good luck!

JOHN WOODEN'S COACHING STATISTICS

INDIANA STATE	WON	LOST	
1946–47	18	7	
1947–48	29	7	
Total	*47*	*14*	*.770 pct*
UCLA			
1948–49	22	7	
1949–50	24	7	
1950–51	19	10	
1951–52	19	12	
1952–53	16	8	
1953–54	18	7	
1954–55	21	5	
1955–56	22	6	
1956–57	22	4	
1957–58	16	10	
1958–59	16	9	
1959–60	14	12	
1960–61	18	8	
1961–62	18	11	
1962–63	20	9	
1963–64*	30	0	
1964–65*	28	2	
1965–66	18	8	
1966–67*	30	0	
1967–68*	29	1	
1968–69*	29	1	
1969–70*	28	2	
1970–71*	29	1	
1971–72*	30	0	
1972–73*	30	0	
1973–74	26	4	
1974–75*	28	3	
Total	*620*	*147*	*.808 pct*

*Indicates NCAA Tournament Champions.

Andy Hill's Playing Statistics

University High	G	PTS	PPG	FGA	FGM	REB	A
1966–67	14	206	14.7	123	57	49	49
1967–68	14	383	27.4	216	120	52	168

UCLA

FRESHMAN

	G	PTS	PPG	FGA	FGM	REB	A
1968–69	18	351	19.5	275	112	97	137

VARSITY

	G	PTS	PPG	FGA	FGM	REB	A
1969–70	24	42	1.8	38	11	15	N/A
1970–71	19	31	1.6	16	7	4	N/A
1971–72	27	71	2.7	45	16	22	N/A